Detachment

The Secret to Infinite Peace

Reclaim your Power and Realise the Truth with the LiberatingTouch® Detachment Process

Ranjana and Eddie Appoo

Copyright

Title: Detachment – The Secret to Infinite Peace
Authors: Ranjana and Eddie Appoo

2nd Kindle Edition Published September 2020
1st Kindle Edition Published in December 2014
© 2020 Ranjana and Eddie Appoo, LiberatingTouch Centre, UK.
Email: liberatingtouchcentre@gmail.com

Cover design, illustrations and photographs by Eddie and Ranjana Appoo

ALL RIGHTS RESERVED. This book contains material protected under International Copyright Laws and Treaties. Any unauthorised reprint or use of this material is prohibited. No part of this book may be reproduced or transmitted in any form or by any means, electronic or mechanical, including photocopying, recording, or by any information storage and retrieval system without express written permission from the author / publisher.

*We offer this book at the Lotus Feet of
Our Beloved Swami
(Bhagawan Sri Sathya Sai Baba)*

Table of Contents

PREFACE 1

    Disclaimer and Release Agreement   5

INTRODUCING_LIBERATINGTOUCH® 7

    About LiberatingTouch®   8

1._DETACHMENT HEALS 13

    What is Detachment?   14

    Sophie's Experience – Healing after a Relationship Break-up   22

    Anna's Experience – Marital Healing   25

2._POWER 27

    Reclaiming Power to Respond with Peace   31

    Grace's Experience—Discovering Love, Freedom, Respect, and Harmony in Family Relationships   37

    Clara's Experience – Coming to terms with where I am Now.   40

Peter's Experience – Using the Detachment Process for Addictions and Anxiety 42

3. INFINITISE, DIVINISE, ... 45

The Elements of the LiberatingTouch® Detachment Process 46

The Liquid Light Relaxation 48

The Tree Meditation for Connecting to the Illumined-Self 48

The Infinity Exercise 49

The Finger Holds 53

The Chakra Meditation 54

Using Light Imagery to Uncreate Energetic Links and Purify the Mind 58

The Tree Integration Meditation 58

Simon's Experience – Using the Infinity Exercise for Exam Stress 60

Jemima's Experience – Creating Honesty and Harmony in all Relationships 62

Angel's Experience – Saying Goodbye 64

4._THE COMPLETE PROCESS 66

The LiberatingTouch® Detachment Process has 4 Main Steps 66

Step 1: Relax, connect and ask the Illumined-Self what to detach from 67

Step 2: Practice the Infinity Exercise with the Finger Holds 75

Step 3: Use the Detachment Visualisation audio or script 79

The Complete Script for the Detachment Visualisation Technique 81

Step 4: Write the Letter to the SELF 95

Important Considerations 96

FREQUENTLY ASKED QUESTIONS 98

An Important Note About the Illumined-Self 114

About Ranjana and Eddie 116

Preface

The *LiberatingTouch*® Detachment Process is one of many *LiberatingTouch*® practical hands-on applications that can help you reclaim power, respond with peace to all of life's challenges, and eventually help you realise the SELF (GOD[1]).

This book has been lovingly written for you and all our family, friends, clients, and students, who have asked (persistently) for a practical hands-on, easy to use, explanatory book, describing the *LiberatingTouch*® Detachment Process. We hope this book fulfils your expectations. We are grateful to you for choosing this book. In the early nineties, when we first embarked on this journey of detachment, Eddie and I discovered Phyllis Krystal's work, "Cutting the Ties that Bind". We are appreciative of her work as we utilised her method for years. In 2009, our Beloved Swami inspired us to create the *LiberatingTouch*® Detachment Process. It is this process that we now practice and teach. We encourage you to read Phyllis Krystal's books as they provide valuable insight and background to this work.

There are many theoretical treatises on the benefits and importance of detachment, but few demonstrate how you can do this. I remember being advised to, *"Let go, forgive, get*

---

[1] 'GOD' refers to consciousness at the level of the Absolute.

over it, move on, accept, live in the present, and so on", and it used to confuse me as I did not know where to begin. How does one let go? In my attempts to unburden this mind, I would exhale till I was hyperventilating! My issues, lack of confidence, illness, addictions, and anxiety, followed me like an undercurrent of toxic discontent, poisoning my body, mind and life. Fortunately, help was at hand and it came in many guises, showing up as Hatha Yoga, Visualisation, Art Therapy, EFT (Emotional Freedom Techniques), 'The Work' of Byron Katie, Phyllis Krystal's 'Cutting the Ties that Bind', Reflexology, Homeopathy, Tapas Acupressure Technique (TAT), Jin Shin Jyutsu, Ayurveda, and Spiritual Healing. Eddie and I have also researched and studied Kinesiology, Crystal healing, Magnet healing, Transpersonal psychology, Zen meditation, Eastern philosophy, Astrology, Sound therapy, Eastern rituals, Chants, Forgiveness processes, NLP (Neuro-linguistic Programming), Numerology, Mudras, Breath-work, Qi Gong, Physical trauma release and many more. Every one of these explorations provided timely answers and insights. We are grateful to every therapist, philosopher, healer, guide, and teacher whom we have studied with and encountered.

After years of practice, research, self-development, experiential wisdom, and inspiration, we created *LiberatingTouch*® and the *LiberatingTouch*® Detachment Process. We do not advocate that this process is better than any of the other processes we have explored. Simply that this is what developed from years of study and inspiration; this is what worked wonderfully for us, our clients, and students.

The *LiberatingTouch*® Detachment Process creates an amazing healing space for the mind so that we can detach from our stories, attitudes and addictions, to reveal the SELF and experience the clarity that comes from constant integrated awareness. Detachment is the secret to infinite peace, liberation and Self-Realisation. It endows us with the ability to live a life that is saturated with Love and Truth[2].

Over the years, Eddie and I have worked with hundreds of clients and we have witnessed these processes used in a multitude of ways to heal and transform. We are continually reminded of how wonderfully effective they are. We have seen the Detachment Process and its elements used for anger management, anxiety issues, financial problems, job insecurity, work pressures, natural disasters, allergies, unfulfilled desires, relationship challenges, fear of public speaking, addictions and even for terminal illness. It is delightfully inspiring to see our clients reclaim their power, discover peace, and be free to grow.

Recently, we heard three accounts that highlighted the scope of these processes. The first one is from a mother,

---

[2] 'Love and Truth' here expresses the quality of 'GOD' or the 'Absolute Self'.

who spoke of how her child had overcome bullying at school, and the child was now teaching her classmates the Infinity Exercise and the Finger Holds. The second account is from a woman, whose husband battled with cancer and died in her arms peacefully, while she drew the Infinity symbol on his chest with rose oil. The third account is from one of our students, who found herself stuck in financial and relationship difficulties. After she completed a few *LiberatingTouch*® Detachment Processes, she was able to clear some of her debt effortlessly and move away from disempowering relationships.

Within these pages you will find a clear outline about how to free your life from the past, release anxieties about the future, and reclaim your power to live contentedly in the present. Nothing that you read here is set in stone; it is open to modification, inspired amendments and further development.

We are deeply grateful to those who have kindly documented their *LiberatingTouch*® Detachment Process experiences, so that we may share their stories with you. To preserve confidentiality, all names and some identifying attributes have been edited. These accounts have been recounted by *LiberatingTouch*® clients and students.

With Love, Ranjana, November 2013

Detachment – The Secret to Infinite Peace

Disclaimer and Release Agreement

LiberatingTouch® is part of an evolving new discipline of treatment techniques and protocols referred to as Energy Therapy. While still considered experimental, therapists, nurses, physicians, psychologists and laypeople worldwide, use these techniques successfully. To date, Energy Therapy Techniques have yielded exceptional results in the treatment of psychological and physical problems. They are NOT, however, meant to replace appropriate medical treatment or mental health therapy. We did not experience any adverse side effects when applying these techniques when the treatment protocols and suggestions were followed. This does not mean that you or your clients will not experience or perceive any side effects. If you use these techniques, download the audios mentioned, and/or try the LiberatingTouch® Sequences on yourself or others, you agree to take full responsibility for your well-being, and you advise your clients to do the same. Before beginning any new health regimen, i.e. diet, exercise, yoga, martial arts, meditation or LiberatingTouch®, check with your doctor or primary care physician.

LiberatingTouch® is founded on ancient philosophy, experiential wisdom, and hands-on investigation; there is no clinical evidence to prove its effectiveness.

We accept no responsibility or liability whatsoever for the use or misuse of the information and audio downloads provided on the website, including but not limited to; LiberatingTouch®, EFT (Emotional Freedom Techniques), Jin Shin Jyutsu, and related activities. By reading or downloading this book, you agree and understand that this Disclaimer is a Release Agreement, and is intended to be a complete unconditional release of liability and assumption of risk, to the greatest extent permitted by law.

Detachment – The Secret to Infinite Peace

Introducing
LiberatingTouch®

"The secret to a life filled with contentment and infinite peace begins with detachment."[3]

There is an old Zen saying, *"Before enlightenment, chop wood, draw water. After enlightenment, chop wood, draw water."* In *LiberatingTouch*® workshops, this precept is paraphrased as, *"Before enlightenment, love and serve, and after enlightenment, love and serve."* The difference is that before enlightenment people love and serve expecting appreciation, approval, or recognition, and their actions are coloured by their attachments. After enlightenment people love and serve without any expectations; their actions come from a place of detachment, and therefore, express the fullness of Love and Truth. The enlightened know the power of detachment, and that is their secret to infinite peace. With the *LiberatingTouch*® Detachment Process, we reveal step-by-step ways to practise detachment and align ourselves with Love and Truth.

---

[3] Any unreferenced quotations in this book are from our private journals or conversations with our students.

This book describes one of the LiberatingTouch® practical applications, which can help you enjoy detachment in daily life. By consistently practising the exercises described in this book, you can access the secret of infinite peace.

About LiberatingTouch®

In today's climate, there seems to be a growing thirst to know how to live life truthfully, peacefully, joyfully and lovingly. How can you put into practice the ancient and esoteric wisdom that is now becoming available? How can you heal the suffering in your mind and illuminate the wisdom in your Heart? How can you let go? How can you be detached and compassionate? How can you reclaim your confidence and power? LiberatingTouch® and its many processes were created to meet this hunger to be free and know contentment. It is the secret to harmonious mental, emotional and physical health.

LiberatingTouch® is a dynamic heart centred process that incorporates Jin Shin Jyutsu, common sense, explorations in subtle energy, investigations into the way the mind stores suffering, EFT (Emotional Freedom Techniques) and the Transformative Power of Love. LiberatingTouch® is a way of uncreating suffering, confusion, judgement, pain, fear, lack of confidence, trauma, and the many wounds of the mind. This enables you to share Truth, Love, Joy, Beauty, Enthusiasm, Compassion and Peace. It has been described as the practical path of Love and Truth.

With *LiberatingTouch®* we understand that healing arises from the SELF[4]. The SELF is consciousness at the level of the Absolute. That is - Omniscient, Omnipresent, Omnipotent, often described as GOD. The term the Illumined-Self in *LiberatingTouch®* describes the intelligence that reflects Love and Truth, from the level of the Absolute (GOD).

As human beings, most people are masters at keeping themselves stuck, and they can reject, or deny the SELF from healing them. Through the *LiberatingTouch®* process, an opening or a shift takes place in consciousness, allowing the innate healing power to manifest.

Quite simply, *LiberatingTouch®* entails connecting to the wisdom within you. With this wisdom, you can get to the crux of whatever is creating disharmony or distress in your life. Through awareness and inquiry, and by stimulating various locations on the face, chest and fingers, the body's energetic makeup is balanced, resulting in the healing of mental-emotional resistance, blocks and suffering.

---

[4] Ranjana and Eddie describe their understanding of the SELF in-depth in the Heart of Understanding Class. Please note that when referring to the persona or ego identity, a lower case 's' is used, as in 'self'. When you see SELF, it signifies GOD (Brahman - The source of Absolute Love and Truth).

Detachment – The Secret to Infinite Peace

The *LiberatingTouch*® features include:

- Connecting to the Universal Illumined SELF **(IS)**
- Creative visualisation
- Touch with awareness
- Breath awareness
- Meditative inquiry
- Intuitive listening
- Utilising body wisdom
- Storytelling
- Comprehending the nature of thoughts and emotions
- Understanding dreams and metaphors
- Sketching
- Music
- Movement
- Eastern philosophy and
- Experiential knowledge of the forces that shape us

LiberatingTouch® enables you to move from patterns of self-destruct to Self-discovery, thereby opening the door to Self-Fulfilment and Self-Realisation.

The purpose of Self-Realisation[5] is to awaken to the Truth of who you are. In knowing the Truth, you will be free

---

[5] Self-Realisation can also be described as becoming conscious (awake) in the SELF beyond the mind.

from ignorance. The ignorance of identifying the SELF with the body or mind will cease.

To truly know the SELF is to know who you truly are, your power and your purpose. *LiberatingTouch®* cleanses and expands the mind, examines attachments and fears, unravels stories, and strengthens your intrinsic faith and Self-confidence. By using the 4 tenets; TRUTH, SELF-RESPONSIBILITY, PEACE, and LOVE, *LiberatingTouch®* illumines the Heart[6] and frees you to be all that you truly are, beyond the constraints of physicality, time and space.

The LiberatingTouch® Processes Reveal:

1. All Wisdom (emerging from Truth) is within you.
2. This Wisdom can be accessed using inquiry, your breath, hands, and nature.
3. Once you discover this Wisdom, you can use the knowing this brings to create harmony and balance, in health, wealth, relationships, i.e. ALL areas of your life.
4. The purpose of connecting to this Wisdom is to realise the SELF and become aware of its Omnipresence, Omniscience and Omnipotence.

---

[6] The capital letter 'H' denotes the spiritual heart and throughout this book, capital letters are used to emphasise spiritual qualities.

The focus of this book is to disseminate the wisdom of detachment; how to practice detachment, reclaim one's power, and know infinite peace. This book combines philosophy, client anecdotes, instruction, allegories and practical applications. It can be compared to a key, if used responsibly, it can open the door to contentment and peace for everyone.

1.
Detachment Heals, Liberates and Empowers

With Detachment There Is ...

Understanding instead of misunderstanding

Listening instead of defending

Seeing instead of projecting

Responding instead of reacting

Accepting instead of controlling

Respecting instead of dominating

Embracing instead of distancing

Honouring instead of deprecating

Allowing instead of expecting

Learning instead of presuming

Unifying instead of dividing

Bowing instead of condescending

Appreciating instead of judging

Intuiting instead of calculating

Trusting instead of worrying

Enjoying instead of preferring

Loving instead of manipulating

Forgiving instead of blaming

What is Detachment?

"For the wheel of existence, the mind is the focal point, the central hub from which all worldly activities emerge. To be able to penetrate this focal point and obtain a vision of the immortal SELF that is beyond, we must cultivate the practice of non-attachment or detachment." — Sri Sathya Sai Baba

In today's fast-paced world, it is easy to feel fragmented and constantly pulled or pushed in many different directions. Instead of experiencing peace, many experience life in pieces. Stressed about time, money, health, relationships; some resort to ingesting addictive substances, some medicate, some push themselves until they collapse, others withdraw from society, and some decide to take responsibility for their well-being. It is this latter group that understand the vital need to create a healthy balance between work and play. They know what to focus on and what to step away from, and what to let go of and what needs determined effort. This group of seekers will find this book useful, and the former, who struggle to experience peace, balance, and Self-confidence, will find that this book could change their life.

Detachment – The Secret to Infinite Peace

Detachment can also be thought of as non-attachment. Non-attachment is when the mind and the senses are not affected by external circumstances, situations, desires and people. It allows you to maintain balance even in the most challenging of situations. The mind obscures the SELF, and therefore, the mind can be described as a veil. It is a veil of ignorance, which keeps you unaware of the magnificent presence of the SELF that is within you. The mind itself is tied down by the sense organs, attitudes, desires, and stories about the phenomenal world, and is bound by these. Thus, one of the first steps in knowing your true SELF is to understand the mind and teach it detachment.

Just as removing the firewood from the fire automatically reduces the conflagration, reducing the energetic links that bind the mind to objects, habits and beliefs automatically frees the awareness to experience the power of the Self.

Detachment is not disassociation, escape, reaction, lack of caring, disinterest, resistance, or denial of feeling, but it is a loving connection. Detachment is the essence of compassion. Detachment allows you to develop an awareness of unity, and know that everything is interconnected by Love and Truth. This knowing can give a depth of purpose and meaning to life. Detachment is the illuminating ability to see all challenging situations and people with clarity and compassion.

In its most potent form, it is surrendering to the SELF (the Source of Empathy, Love and Forgiveness).

Detachment allows you to live in the present, free to make empowered choices, to focus on harmony and avoid getting entangled in unnecessary drama and stress. It gives clear vision, so even in the most difficult situations, you can come from a place of power, inner confidence and peace. These energetic ties can keep you stuck in a tug of war; in a constant state of push-pull and intolerant relationships. Wouldn't you like to end the war and free yourself from the web of limitations and fear?

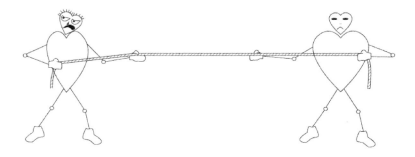

Do you find that you are not being heard? Do you get defensive? Do you need to be right? Do you feel inadequate in your relationships? Do you react with anger regularly? Are you afraid of being rejected, abandoned and alone? Are you attached to your parents or grown-up children? Are you addicted to unhealthy substances? Do you need an alcoholic drink at the end of every day? When you look in the mirror do you wince? Are your thoughts about yourself harsh, unkind or judgmental? Are your relationships a tug of war? If you answer yes to any of these questions, then the *LiberatingTouch*® Detachment Process will serve you well. It will help you uncreate the energetic ties and conditioned behaviour that keeps you stuck in unhealthy patterns.

The origins of these patterns are discussed in detail, in the *LiberatingTouch*® 'Heart of Understanding Class'. There are many reasons why these conditions manifest, and they are too numerous to list here. What is significant, is knowing (becoming aware) that you do not need to be stuck in negative repetitive behaviour. Some people believe that they cannot be free and that they are enmeshed permanently in the tragic situations they find themselves in. They believe that their unhappy relationships and lives are the way things are and that there is no escape from misery and stress, for suffering is all there is. But what if it was possible, even in the most difficult circumstances to find peace? What if you could dive deep into that well of Truth that exists in every heart, and experience that Love? What if the energetic links could be uncreated and you could find your voice? What if you could be free to discover your inner compass? What if you did not need to live in the shadow of the past? What if you did not need to repeat the errors or prejudice of your parents? What if you could heal the sorrow and fear? What if you could find peace?

A Story

"Have you ever heard yourself say, 'That's my story and I am sticking to it'? Well, perhaps it is time to 'unstick' yourself if you want to experience the freedom of an open mind."

Attachments and desires anchor people in misunderstanding and suffering. Attachments to family, friends, opinions, beliefs, certainty, and security, are all hurdles in the search for Truth. Desires for safety, pleasure, comfort, appreciation, approval, respect, and recognition, although perfectly understandable, can make people fearful and insecure. People can become controlling, anxious, and even exhausted in their attempts to keeping up appearances. When we create a positive habit of detachment, we cultivate the ability to acknowledge our desires, needs, stories and expectations with Love and Truth. Detachment is not about avoiding discomfort, but facing stress, resentment, awkwardness, and insecurity with honesty and fearless self-acceptance. This power to face all facets of life is liberating.

Desires and attachments delude people into identifying with the material world and keep them from perceiving, the infinite possibilities at their fingertips.

Here is an allegorical story about a student who wanted to understand the nature of how attachment deludes, and why people can get caught up in the belief that their stories and identifications are real.

The student tenaciously asked his teacher, over and over, the same questions: "What is the nature of attachment? Why is it deluding? How can I be free from the delusion?" The teacher avoided answering these questions for years. He found ways to sidestep his student's persistent queries, either with silence, by diverting his attention or laughing. As the years passed, the student did not let up, and at every opportunity, he asked his teacher the same questions.

Then one crisp autumn day, the teacher and student were walking in the woods. Suddenly, the teacher let out a huge cry, ran up to an old large tree stump, grabbed it and started yelling, "Help, help, help, I am trapped. Help me. The tree stump will not let me go. I am stuck. The stump has got me, HELP!!" The student was utterly bewildered by the teacher's actions. He ran to the teacher and tried to pry him away from the tree stump, but the teacher held onto the stump even tighter. The student did not know what to do as the teachers' wails got even louder, and nothing the student said or did made any difference. The teacher had adhered himself to the stump, and then yelled that the stump had captured him!! At first, the student started to doubt his teacher's sanity, but then seeing the teacher so distressed, he began to believe that the stump had somehow overwhelmed and ensnared his teacher. The confused student began to cry. At this, the teacher freed his arms from the stump, dusted his clothes, straightened himself out, and walked away.

The student was completely baffled. He ran after his teacher and asked him, "What just happened?" The teacher smiled and said, "That is the nature of attachment. With our thinking and senses we get enmeshed in the world around us, and then believe that the created world has entangled us. The only way to be free is to realise the TRUTH. To know, that we are and have always been free. You, my dear student, because of your attachment to me, forgot the truth that it was I who ran to the stump and attached myself. The stump had no power over me. By forgetting the truth, you believed the delusion that I had created."

This story demonstrates that people have chosen to believe in their powerlessness and suffering, and they can choose to investigate and detach from these untruths. The best place to begin on this journey of detachment is to understand the nature of power and how you can reclaim your personal power to access the Cosmic Power within you.

Sophie's Experience – Healing after a Relationship Break-up

"I chose to try the LiberatingTouch® Detachment Process because I was feeling very sad at the end of my relationship with my long-term partner David. We had been a couple for fifteen years, on and off, and despite living together I had become increasingly lonely and isolated. I had a great fear of ending the relationship as I was invested in it being successful, and we did love each other. However, neither of us could move towards a full commitment and David was also suffering from depression. I too despaired because I couldn't see a way forward for us, so finally, I decided to move out and hopefully move on.

For the first few weeks, I stayed upbeat by keeping busy and dealing with the practicalities of such a big change. Fearing my feelings, I did all I could to keep them at bay. I dreaded the sensation of a 'black hole' depression that I had previously experienced when we had parted. Feeling abandoned and frightened, I was also aware of my co-dependence. I had left the relationship to be content, peaceful and free of the day-to-day negative dramas, yet I found I was still obsessing about our past and the 'if only's'. I felt very low.

With such a sense of loss and hurt, it was hard to function. I felt traumatised by the events of the past few years and had lost sight of a loving relationship with mutual goodwill and respectful empowerment. Angry with myself for the self-sacrifice, I could see that I had not served David's best interest by being silent; I could have spoken up and accounted for myself. He had been a perfect mirror of my shadow-side, and I learnt huge lessons in our time spent together.

Ranjana gave me renewed hope and restored my trust and faith. When she suggested the LiberatingTouch® Detachment Process, I didn't expect much change and was rather nervous that it would make life harder before things would get better. For this reason, I was a bit reluctant to put it into practice, but at the same time, I had a sense it was right for me to do.

What surprised me was how the process uncovered layers of past trauma. I could feel years of discomfort peeling away within myself. I felt very vulnerable and, at the same time, I received vast amounts of love and understanding. For the first time in my life, I found myself reaching out and asking for help. I could feel some part of me waking up properly and seeing the bigger picture. I began to appreciate the joy in chance encounters when travelling or meeting people in connection with my work. As a result, I now feel super-connected at the heart-level with clients, and cherish friendships and family in a new way.

The process made me aware. It was amazing how much grief I had stored. I would arrive at Ranjana's door thinking my sad days were behind me, but the grief would surface in a way I had not expected. It felt as if it came from the depths of the wounded areas throughout my body-mind. The release was always powerful and would leave me lighter, more optimistic.

After I had completed the Detachment Process with David, I felt different in a subtle way. The real test came when I went back to the house to collect some possessions. My initial emotional reaction didn't have the same charge, and I could see clearly. I was able to self-soothe and deal with the meeting in a much less reactive way. I also recovered quickly and didn't feel the need to be in contact with him. This was a huge change, and I feel I can take care of myself now.

The next detachment I was inspired to undertake was to 'the critical mother energy' inside me. Perhaps, this is why I was attracted to the partners I chose as most of them seemed to be critical of me. Sadly, David played this part and added to my low self-esteem and lack of confidence. Throughout my childhood, I had never felt I 'made the grade' and this has been a burden throughout my life, affecting all areas of my experience. I used to feel immense anxiety all the time at the thought of getting it wrong or making a mistake. Happily, with a mixture of understanding and humour, Eddie and Ranjana were able to help me release a tremendous amount of built-up anger, in particular at myself.

Dealing with 'the critical mother energy' has had a profound effect on my well-being and the benefits are on-going. Interestingly, my actual mother (who is elderly) is now noticeably less critical and much more appreciative. When we had to go to the hospital, she commented on how much she liked my company and how pleased she was to see me. She made a point of telling me she loved me, how she wanted the best for my future and to see me settled. It felt really wonderful. I likewise felt a genuine pleasure at being able to assist her and look after her.

I am really happy I used LiberatingTouch®, and I am grateful for the many positive changes in my life. I am experiencing new, kinder relationships. I'm taking a few more risks and feel I am emerging into a brighter future, with the help of Grace. My prayer is to surrender to that Illumined Power and just be myself."

Anna's Experience — Marital Healing

"I began working with Ranjana and using the Detachment Process because my life was a bit of a mess with marital tension, work issues and, on top of those, family and money problems. I can't recall what I detached from the first time! I remember doing the exercises and not being able to concentrate because of my marital problems. I remember writing the letter and burning it, but for the life of me, I have no idea what I wrote. Ranjana let me know that this is normal: sometimes the issue has been resolved so thoroughly, it is as if it never existed.

The most recent one I did was to 'bones'. At the beginning of the exercise, I saw an image of actual bones that showed up in the Infinity Symbol. I had no idea what these bones meant. I simply trusted the Illumined-Self was guiding me and that I needed to detach from this energy, whatever it might be. As I practised the Infinity Exercise, the image of bones became the word 'bones' and, towards the end of the two weeks, the word 'bones' became three-dimensional.

While practising Step 2 of the LiberatingTouch® Detachment Process (the Infinity Exercise and Finger Holds), I had a lot of tears during the first couple of days. Things weren't so good and got worse for the first ten days or so. Then the day before doing the guided visualisation step of the Detachment Process with Ranjana, I watched a film of my childhood and it dawned on me that I had all this pent-up anger and was suffering a lot because of my experience with my parents. I realised that this anger had created a shadow over my entire life.

Step 3 was excellent. Ranjana did a fab job, and I was so astonished with all the rage that came out of me. The letter wouldn't burn and, when finally, it did, I could see a snippet remaining and so lit it again. After the session, I looked again and there was still a little piece left! Once it was completed, everything improved.

There has been a lovely change between me and my husband. Things are much calmer now, and the relationship between us is getting better every day. We even laugh together (it hasn't been like this for a long time). I feel a lot calmer also, and I am being kinder to myself. I have learnt to trust the process that it's not necessary to understand what the symbol means. Why 'bones' was the symbol that my Self revealed to me, I still don't know. I am looking forward to doing the next Detachment Process."

2.
Power

"We are not victims, but powerful beyond measure. Even if we forget this, and circumstances, memories, or thoughts keep us replaying the roles of a victim, we can always wake up from this trance of material identification. We can reconnect to the Truth. We can shine the light of awareness, dispelling the darkness of our fears and illuminating the infinite power of the Heart. We can shake off the lies of powerlessness like a lion shakes his mane, and roar with the certainty that we are formidable."

One of the preliminary steps towards Self-Realisation is to work towards the infinite power within each one of us. This infinite power is also known as the divine Cosmic Power. What is this Cosmic Power? The Cosmic Power pervades the entire universe and is not different from that in man. The sun derives its energy from this Cosmic source. It is the same Cosmic source that accounts for the power of the human mind and the marvellous power of the eye to see the most distant stars. Even though invisible, it is like electricity flowing in a cable, which is only apparent when one switches on the light, appearing dimmer or brighter depending on the wattage of the light bulb. This boundless power is recognised and exercised by each one according to the level of his or her development. Just as the same electrical energy is used for a variety of purposes, for example, heating, lighting etc. likewise, the divine Cosmic energy in human beings is used by different individuals for varied purposes. This energy is latent in all beings. How do we[7] manifest this divine Cosmic energy? We have to start by building up our personal power.

Personal Power

> *"First develop your personal power, and then you will begin to recognise the Truth and access the universal divine power that pervades everything. We are energetic beings of infinite power and potential; we are the perfection of all that we seek."*

This is the power we use to accomplish our daily living, and any other pursuits or endeavours imbued with our intellectual knowledge or physical strength. Our lives are influenced by beliefs and conditions that help or hinder us at every turn, even though we are not always aware that we have

---

[7] In this chapter 'we' is used to indicate (include) both the author and the reader.

created them ourselves. These beliefs and conditions are the cause of self-sabotage, and no one is to blame, even though we consistently point our 'finger of blame' at others. We have created, by habitual and usually negative behaviour patterns, filters within our mind that cause us to behave in a way not consistent with our own truth. For example, we may lie because the 'filter of fear' makes us shy away from the consequences of our actions. This, in turn, adds more energy to fearful thinking, which takes from us our self-confidence, and our power. We have many such conditions that we have inherited or created from our childhood that has taken our power away from us.

Most of us believe that we have finite power; we have only intellectual power or physical power. So, we work within the constraints of our belief system. How do we recognise that our belief systems are false? If we have an experience that runs counter to our own belief systems, would we still hold that belief to be true? For example, there are instances where a mother lifted a car or other heavy object to save her child trapped underneath it. In normal circumstances, even a very strong man would be unable to lift it. The ability of the mother to accomplish that feat is purely the result of the suspension of her belief system that it was beyond her ability. We have conditioned ourselves to believe that we are weak and powerless, but we are infinitely more powerful than we dare believe. When we come into our personal power, we also become true to our SELF. Then, we won't feel the need to control anyone, as TRUTH need not defend itself.

We need to reclaim our personal power in order to connect to the Cosmic Power. This will help us recognise that we are not confined to time and space; we are neither the body nor the thoughts that come and go. This self-empowerment helps open our awareness to the Cosmic Power within us. We are limitless consciousness experiencing a dream born of infinite love emerging from Truth.

What Happened to Your Power?

"Detachment is the spiritual warrior's armour."

Personal power is the energy manifesting in this life that we have brought over, as a result of the loss or gains we made over many lives, by locking them up in other objects and desires. Using a banking analogy, we could say for example, that we had a million pounds sterling in our current account. Over the course of many lives, we have created many smaller accounts (attachment to family members, possessions etc.) where we have transferred various amounts from the current account until our current account has dwindled so much that we become powerless. The money is still there (in the smaller accounts) but we cannot access it. We need this money (energy) to connect to the Cosmic Power. Only by becoming detached from the conditioned behaviour or pattern, can we bring the money or energy back to our current account. Detachment is the most effective way to reclaim our spiritual wealth and power.

Reclaiming Power to Respond with Peace

"Detachment allows you to enjoy every moment, relationship, and activity, free from insecure possessive thinking."

Once we become aware of how our attachments and fears compromise our power, we can take responsibility. We can use the elements of the *LiberatingTouch*® Detachment Process or use the complete process to reclaim our power. As we regain our power using these processes, we integrate our experiences and feel confident in the SELF, and therefore, respond to all of life with peace.

The First Stage in Reclaiming Personal Power is Awareness.

We can begin by asking ourselves where we have given away our power. We can start by making a list of all the issues (challenges) we have. This will help us pinpoint the areas

Detachment – The Secret to Infinite Peace

where we have given away our power. This can be difficult for some, as they are not used to being aware. So many are in denial about how they consistently sabotage healing, relationships, success, and opportunities for growth, and peace. If this step is a struggle, it is a good idea to book a session with a *LiberatingTouch*® Facilitator[8].

Here are some common examples of how we lose power:

- Attachments (to family/friends/comfort/ objects/ familiarity/opinions/judgements)
- Fear and Anger
- Accumulation and clutter
- Lying/dishonesty
- Addictions
- Giving too much personal information away
- Anxiety
- Being excessively apologetic
- Having excessive desires
- Malice or hatred
- Envy
- Vows/decisions made to avoid suffering
- Debt
- Either reliving or blanking out memories
- Shame and guilt

---

[8] Go to www.liberatingtouch.com to find a LiberatingTouch Facilitator

To open our awareness of where and how we lose power, we can cradle the front and back of our head with the *LiberatingTouch*® R&R Hold, (as illustrated below), while saying the following words: *"Although it is hard for me to pinpoint all the areas where I lose power, I am open to being aware."*

Simply make a note of whatever shows up. By approaching life with awareness, we can make new and different decisions about what we want to create. Sometimes a shift in perception seems to be all we need to allow changes to take effect in our life.

The Second Stage in Reclaiming Personal Power is Taking Responsibility.

Taking responsibility with compassion, with kindness, without blame, without denigration, helps us understand why we did what we did, and accept that errors or mistakes were made and simply need resolution. This gives us the opportunity to recognise that we can choose and reclaim our power, or not.

To open to an experience of responsible wisdom cradle the front and back of the head with the *LiberatingTouch*® R&R Hold, while saying the following words: *"It is hard for me to accept my mistaken perceptions and errors; I am now ready to take responsibility compassionately."*

The Third Step in Reclaiming Personal Power is Loving Action

This is where the *LiberatingTouch*® Detachment Process and its elements play a vital part. It is at this stage, when we need to take action that most resistance to healing is encountered.

To release some of this resistance, cradle the front and back of the head with the *LiberatingTouch*® R&R Hold while saying the following words: *"Even though I resist taking loving action and stepping into my power, I am open to experiencing Cosmic Power."*

Detachment – The Secret to Infinite Peace

Below are some practical applications that we can use to reclaim our power (detailed in the following two chapters):

- The Tree Meditation for connecting to the Illumined-Self
- The Infinity Exercise
- The Finger Holds
- The complete *LiberatingTouch*® Detachment Process

The Final Stage in Reclaiming Personal Power is Integration

As we detach from that which has been draining our power, we also begin to notice harmony in our thoughts, words and actions. We begin to come into our power and experience equanimity. We notice changes in our own behaviour and feedback from others reflects this. We open to the acceptance and understanding that everything is temporary, and change happens all the time. We begin to embrace the strength that comes from knowing we can meet all situations with serenity. Even if we feel agitated, disturbed, and helpless, we can always detach, connect to Truth, and respond with peace.

Often during this phase of integration, people notice that they slip back into old behaviour patterns or that they get overwhelmed or stressed by old triggers. They hope that the healing work that they have done to date is sufficiently liberating. It can come as a surprise that there is always more to detach from, more to learn, more to resolve, more to forgive, more to integrate, and more to love.

To maintain the experience of gratitude that integration brings, cradle the front and back of the head with the *LiberatingTouch*® R&R Hold while saying the following words: "Although I may slip back into old patterns, I now know how to reclaim my power. I thank the SELF for this peace, wisdom and integration."

Having read this chapter on power, imagine what our life would be like if we could detach successfully, and reclaim our power? In the following chapters, there are detailed descriptions of the elements of the *LiberatingTouch*® Detachment Process and the complete process.

Grace's Experience—Discovering Love, Freedom, Respect, and Harmony in Family Relationships

"My father, aged 75, was diagnosed with cancer. I wanted to make peace with him and my mother, but found myself wanting to 'control' his treatment regime, both medical and complementary. Being a holistic practitioner, I believed that if my father could engage with the emotional processes that I had faith in, he would be better able to cope with his illness and get to the root cause. He did try some of the techniques and found them relaxing, but on the whole, he did not want to explore the emotional contributors to his condition. It was difficult seeing him get frustrated, angry and withdrawn as he was normally quite cheerful. My mother was also struggling with the situation. Having taken on the chief carers' role, I began to realise that I was getting too close to the outcome. I wanted to let go and be more accepting of my father's choice of treatment, whether it was medical, complementary, emotional, spiritual, or some combination of these. After working on myself with EFT (Emotional Freedom Techniques), Journeywork, and LiberatingTouch®, I was able to accept his chosen path, and yet our relationship continued to be strained. It was evident that our values did not concur. I was constantly preoccupied with his physical, and emotional, and spiritual wellbeing.

When I learnt of the LiberatingTouch® Detachment Process, I resolved to detach from my father and mother. However, when I connected with the Illumined-Self, via the Tree, I was shown Lord Krishna in the other loop which did not make sense to me. That was when Ranjana asked what my son's *name was, and it was indeed one of Lord Krishna's names. I saw from this that the challenges I had been facing with my son had been covered over by the current focus on my father. Although I was desperate to detach from my father and mother, I had been guided to perform the more necessary detachment to my son first. Ranjana advised me that it is best to follow the dictates of the Illumined-Self as it has a more encompassing perspective.*

During this detachment process, my son telephoned (from the other side of the world) indicating that he had some real issues that he wanted to talk to me about. This was no coincidence. My son's call reinforced my sense that the choice for the detachment process had been the right one! That call was one of many timely confirmations to come my way in the following days. The whole process was quite full-on as my son called and messaged me regularly that week, something that was truly unexpected. Normally, he would not confide in me or want guidance on the phone unless it was an emergency. At the same time, I began to open to being vulnerable, and let go of control. It felt like there was more turmoil in my life than usual, and I had restless sleep.

The outcome of my son's detachment process was a healthier relationship with him. I accepted the truth that he is a bright, young, and capable adult. Without the clinginess, or the neediness, I realised that parents could have a free, open, flowing, loving relationship with their children. Now, I could love my son unconditionally. The energetic charge and tension that had been there between us had diminished. Things were more relaxed between us. Previously, there had been little communication, and whenever we spoke, there was an underlying tone of anger and resentment. Now things are effortless, less anxious – we're not on tippy toes anymore! There are times when there is friction, yes; but it is far less severe. A quick Infinity Exercise with him fixes it! There are none of the on-going negative emotions that were common before. Now we have mutual respect for each other's choices.

Soon after, I noticed that my daughter was now the one that was feeling 'left out', and she was quite bitter about our relationship. More tension developed between my daughter and son. In response, I used the Infinity Exercise as a surrogate between the two of them whenever a conflicting situation arose. Having completed the detachment with my son, I wanted to detach from my daughter, father and mother. I really wanted freedom now! Yet the process taught me that I need to be patient. There is an intricate design to life, and certain things need to be loosened first before one can tackle what one is keen to release and free.

I subsequently did two other detachments before I was finally guided to detach from my father, and then my mother. Once completed, the processes freed both my father and me, and my mother and me, to respect each other's choices and to live in harmony.

Later I was guided to detach from my daughter, this too was an intense process, and initially, things got so much worse between us. Ranjana's guidance and reassurance helped me to remain focused, and on track when I was anxious about my relationship with my daughter. Now, I realise that surrendering to the truth produces a positive outcome according to divine timing and not necessarily when I want it! It is wonderfully fulfilling when as a family we can allow each other to be authentic, empowered, and able to communicate with love and equanimity. It is a joy to be cultivating relationships based on truth and love."

Clara's Experience – Coming to terms with where I am Now.

When I did a detachment process recently, much had been going on for me; sadness that my daughter is ill and is not speaking with me (or others), anger at my neighbours for creating so much drama, my ageing, as I am past 71 this year... As we entered into the visualization, I saw myself as a flame and heard I was to detach from a sense of self. Initially, my mind started filling in the blanks... with a variety of issues, my daughter, ageing, not being willing to accept help, and of course the thorny problem with my neighbours. Again, I clearly heard "sense of self" ... but didn't understand what it meant. I found a willingness to simply go with this process. I saw the flame of my Illumined Self in one loop of the infinity circle, and an empty, to me, sense of self, in the other loop, with the serpent of light separating them.

Ranjana suggested I was going through a "minusing" of the ego being a cloth with threads that were unravelling. Having some holes in the fabric of "my existence" as I know it, but still no clear understanding of what exactly I was to release...

I did the visualization each day, having faith in the process more than what my mind said. As I wrote the letter of gratitude, I became aware that it was my need to be right, that was the sense of the small self being released. Moving from a layer of the personal into the impersonal, a widening circle which included my family and my community.

As I look back, I find the tension with my neighbours settled of its own accord, it just kind of fizzled out...

> *I experienced increased acceptance of my daughter current situation, allowing me to support whatever decisions she feels are helpful for her, without concern or worry. As for ageing, this is a work in process, receiving help is becoming easier for me, so help shows up more often and I feel grateful. Out of this sense of gratitude, I'm finding gifts that previously were unavailable. Like the joy of a stranger getting an item of the top shelves in the market, something that had once been my role, now the universe is putting me on the receiving end. Making things sweeter and gentler in this fast-paced world.*

Peter's Experience – Using the Detachment Process for Addictions and Anxiety

"I have done more Detachment Processes than I can remember. At one stage, I was doing one a month. It was hard on my partner as the processes often brought up a fair amount of hidden anger, insecurity and sadness. I would then project these on to my partner. Fortunately, my partner had been forewarned and was well versed in the Detachment Process. When the going got rough, my partner reminded me that the 'rough' is temporary. The benefits of these processes are unbelievable. It has given me clarity and a deep sense of peace.

I have used the LiberatingTouch® Detachment Process to detach from my father, mother, siblings, friends and business associates as well as from addictive behaviour patterns, traumas, nightmares, depression, financial concerns, distressing memories, desires, repetitive thoughts, shame, guilt, smoking, alcohol, and even chocolate. I used to feel overburdened with guilt in relation to my family, and so would behave reactively. The processes have helped me to communicate honestly, create good boundaries and develop both integrity and congruence. After completion, not all my relationships were perfect, harmonious and without conflict; but I now had the power to listen and follow my intuition, as opposed to getting swayed by emotional manipulation. The freedom to be able to say "Yes" or "No" from a place of honesty was liberating. In terms of my eating habits, the Detachment Process has helped me make better choices, or at least to be kind to myself when I do not. Each completed process gave me deeper insight.

I remember when I detached from cigarettes, I realised how disempowering smoking was for me. I had seen cigarettes as my one friend in a menacing world, when in fact, they were quite the opposite. The detachment did not automatically free me from ever wanting to smoke, but it did make me want to give up and it cleared all my resistance to living a smoke-free life. It also gave me the strength and conviction to pursue my desire to be healthy. I also used the other LiberatingTouch® processes to help me heal the reasons for needing this 'crutch' in the first place: EFT (Emotional Freedom Techniques) for the cravings, and Jin Shin Jyutsu to clear the body of the stored toxins from years of smoking. One could say that the detachment made it easy for me to deal with something that I had struggled with for a very long time.

For me, the most powerful element of the process is the Infinity Exercise (incorporated in Step 2 of the LiberatingTouch® Detachment Process). I use this at least five or six times a day to help me stay centred and respond with peace to all situations. If I feel stressed, I 'infinitise' it. For example, I used to loathe going to the dentist; now I simply 'infinitise' my anxiety, the dentist and any fears that I have. This takes the edge off. During appointments, I hold my fingers; this relaxes me and my dental experiences are almost agreeable.

I like to explore what is possible with all that I practise. Once, when I was travelling by air, I became aware of a baby crying in great distress. I looked over and noticed the mother was also very distressed. I thought I would try a surrogate version of the Infinity Exercise. I imagined the baby in one loop, and the words 'reason for stress' in the other loop, whilst holding my fingers at the same time. I was surprised when after a few minutes the baby had calmed down and gone to sleep. The mother also seemed more rested. Did the surrogate Infinity Exercise and the Finger Holds help the baby? I have no way of really knowing; I do know it helped me. I have tried this surrogate technique in other circumstances and have always had good results. However, the best results are when I use the Infinity Exercise for myself."

3.
Infinitise, Divinise, Harmonise, Realise

"To the maladies distressing the mind caused by attachment and fear, detachment is both the sharp scalpel of Truth required to remove disorders and the soothing balm of Love's healing touch."

Practising the *LiberatingTouch*® Detachment Process and its elements helps you to Infinitise, Divinise, Harmonise, and Realise. To **Infinitise**, is to use the Infinity Exercise. It is the process of creating space, getting clear, centred, and awakening into non-reactionary awareness.

To **Divinise,** is to pay attention to your thoughts, words, and actions, with kindness. This awareness arises naturally after practising the Infinity Exercise. Infinitising heralds the divinising of our beliefs, emotions and expressions.

To **Harmonise**, is to align your thoughts, words and actions with Love and Truth. You can bring harmony to all areas of your life by using the elements of the *LiberatingTouch*® Detachment Process.

To **Realise**, is to know the SELF; to know the TRUTH.

This process of infinitising, divinising, harmonising and realising occurs gradually as we practise the elements of the *LiberatingTouch*® Detachment Process.

The Elements of the LiberatingTouch® Detachment Process

The *LiberatingTouch*® Detachment Process unites you with Love and Truth through inquiry, visualisation, meditation and energy medicine, so that you can see clearly whatever controls you, or holds you back.

This process has been developed to help you, when you feel stuck and unable to move into your power; unable to express your potential, or are simply unhappy with any aspect of your life. Stuck or trapped energies and attitudes could be attributed to conditioned behaviour patterns, outmoded identifications, critical and negative perceptions of the world, addictions, stressful relationships, illness, disappointment or difficult working conditions.

Detachment – The Secret to Infinite Peace

The *LiberatingTouch*® Detachment Process comprises of:

- The Liquid Light Relaxation
- The Tree Meditation for connecting to the Illumined-Self
- The Infinity Exercise
- The Finger Holds
- The Chakra Meditation
- Using Light Imagery to uncreate energetic links and purify the mind
- The Tree Integration Meditation for balancing, aligning, and being nourished by the Cosmic Masculine and Feminine Energies

Each of the elements listed above is beneficial even when practised separately or in combination, as each element fulfils a particular task. When all these elements are combined as in the complete *LiberatingTouch*® Detachment Process, they enable you to reclaim your power successfully. Regular use of these processes can help you live harmoniously from a place of peace, clarity and truth.

The Liquid Light Relaxation

This visualisation is employed in most LiberatingTouch® individual and group sessions. It relaxes the body-mind and creates a space to dive deep within your consciousness. This shifts the awareness from thinking to intuiting and prepares for the deeper insights that come from connecting to the Illumined-Self. It is also a useful exercise to practise before going to sleep.

The Tree Meditation for Connecting to the Illumined-Self

This visualisation is employed in most LiberatingTouch® individual and group sessions. It is a central feature in

LiberatingTouch® and is discussed in-depth, in the Heart of Understanding 8 Day Class. This is used in both Step 1 and Step 3 of the *LiberatingTouch®* Detachment Process for connecting to the Illumined-Self so that the journey of detachment is guided by the illuminating authority of divine wisdom. By connecting to the Tree, you are connecting to the Illumined-Self (the intelligence that reflects absolute Love and Truth).

The Infinity Exercise

The 'Infinity Exercise' is part of the *LiberatingTouch®* Detachment Process. It is a visualisation technique, in which you visualise or imagine that you are in one loop of a large Infinity Symbol and the object, symbol or person that you need to detach from is in the opposite loop of the Infinity Symbol. You then visualise a 'white serpent of light' moving along the path of the Infinity Symbol (in any direction), looping around you and then looping around the opposite loop, as illustrated in the diagram.

The mind is extremely powerful and thoughts can manifest energetically (as you think so it becomes). When you think of the 'white serpent of light' moving along the path of the Infinity Symbol, in a clockwise direction in front of you in your visualisation, then a vortex spinning in a clockwise direction will be created. When it comes round the loop you

49

are sitting or standing in, it will create another vortex moving in an anticlockwise direction around you. Thus, two energetic vortices will be created, spinning in opposite directions. Physics tells us that objects spinning in opposite directions cannot come together, but will pull apart. A vortex will also pull everything to its centre, just like water in a sink which spirals to the centre as it drains out.

When you do this exercise, you are communicating to the subconscious mind, in symbolic language, to deprogram your attachment to the object, person, or symbol, in the loop opposite you. Therefore, the subconscious will free the energy locked in the conditioned process and allow you to reclaim your power. In effect, it is breaking the pattern of control (fear). This way both parties are liberated from the reactive forces of expectation (desire) and control (fear).

This exercise can be used whenever you feel that you are reacting to someone or something, even during a phone call, or when conversing with someone in person. All you have to do is put yourself in one loop of the Infinity Symbol, and the person or object in the other loop and visualise the 'white serpent of light' going along the path of the Infinity Symbol, till your reaction stops or till you calm down.

This one visualisation can help you at any time to create space so that you can respond to any situation or person with clarity and strength. It is easy to get enmeshed in irate conversations, be triggered by a remark, or to feel pressured. If in that moment, you remember to visualise, think, or even trace the Infinity Symbol with your fingers, imagining that you are in one loop and the person or situation is in the other loop, you can instantly create the breathing space you require to disengage from the story and take inspired action. The use of the Infinity Exercise is also referred to as 'infinitising'.

The Power of Infinitising

There are times in your life when it seems like there is nothing you can do, and everything is falling apart around you. Whichever way you turn, there is tension and hassle. What if in such a moment you could find a place of calm? There is a well-known Zen story that illustrates this. Many Zen stories are open-ended stories. An open-ended story is an invitation to see your situation from a fresh perspective. Unlike conventional stories, there is no specific moral or lesson to learn. It can be enjoyed for itself, or help interpret an actual situation in a new way. In this sense, it is not an intellectual exercise, but an opportunity, to see if any ideas resonate within you. Furthermore, as time and conditions change an individual may see it from a different perspective. Here is the story of "The Tigers and the wild berry".

A man walking across an open field when a tiger suddenly appeared and began to give chase. Although the man ran as fast as he could, the tiger began to close in. As he came to a chasm at the edge of the field, the man grabbed a vine and climbed down the chasm. Holding on as tight as he could, he looked up and saw the angry tiger prowling out of range, ten feet above him. He looked down, and in the gully below there were two more angry tigers also growling and prowling. He had to wait it out. He looked up again and saw that two mice, one white and the other black, had come out of the bushes and began gnawing on the vine, his lifeline. As they chewed the vine, it started to fray, and he knew that it could break at any time. Then growing just an arm's length away the man saw a single wild berry. Holding the vine with one hand, he reached out and picked the wild berry and put it in his mouth. It was sweet and delicious.

Detachment – The Secret to Infinite Peace

There is often a desire to find a way out of your predicaments or dilemmas. Sometimes there are no solutions and it is easy to forget that within the limitations of the moment, there is freedom. In this story, it's the experience of the taste of the wild berry. It reminds you that you can see your situation from a fresh perspective, and live in the moment. The practice of infinitising gives you the space to be present and open, to respond and to any quandary with peace.

The Finger Holds

The Finger Holds are utilised in every *LiberatingTouch*® individual and group session. They play a vital part. By holding the fingers with awareness, you can harmonise all your energy flows. Many ancient cultures and shamanic traditions believe that everyone has an 'energy body' and that energy flows through the body as rivers of vital life force. They believed that when this energy flow is out of balance, it will result in illness, suffering or pain. In *LiberatingTouch*®, this understanding of energy is combined with self-inquiry, self-investigation and self-knowledge, to heal the mind and reveal the immense wisdom of the Heart.

Engaging the healing energy with/in the hands is practised in most ancient healing traditions, for e.g. in Ayurveda and Jin Shin Jyutsu. If you would like to learn more

53

about this, the Jin Shin Jyutsu self-help workshops are a great starting point. By studying Jin Shin Jyutsu, you can learn about the Finger Holds, Energy Balancing Locations, and how one can use them to enhance physical, cognitive and emotional acuity.

By amalgamating this understanding of the energy body and the nature of the mind, you deepen your awareness and access your innate healing potential (see pages 76-78).

The Chakra Meditation

Step 3 of The *LiberatingTouch*® Detachment Process incorporates the Chakra Meditation[9]. It has been added to the process to assist you in raising your vibration so that you have the energy required to complete this process.

The understanding and experiential wisdom of the 'Chakras' are part of Eastern tradition, primarily in India. It is written in many sacred texts, that the deep cleansing and subsequent transformation and transcendence of the mind occur naturally when the energy known as the 'Kundalini'[10] (divine serpent power) is awakened. This divine power - 'Kundalini' then rises through the spinal column opening the 7

---

[9] The Chakra Meditation that Eddie and Ranjana share here comes from their personal experience.
[10] Eddie and Ranjana have had direct experiences of the 'Kundalini', and subsequent experiences of God-Consciousness.

types of lotuses known as Naadi Mandalas or Chakras (Nerve centres or dynamic disks of power) and activates the potential of the divine within the individual. Kundalini, called by various names, seems to have been a universal phenomenon in esoteric teachings for thousands of years. Kundalini-type descriptions or experiences are found in ancient Indian sacred writings (The Vedas), esoteric teachings of the Egyptians, Tibetans, Chinese, some Native Americans, and the Bushmen of Africa. The power of Kundalini has been described as the 'Holy Ghost' in Christianity and is also referenced in the Koran, the works of Plato and other Greek philosophers, and in Hermetic and Kabbalistic writings.

There are seven main chakras or energy vortices[11] that serve to raise the vibration of the body-mind, helping the spiritual aspirant to experience heightened states of awareness. These chakras are power centres, which once activated by the Kundalini to their full potential, reveal the immeasurable power available to everyone. All the chakras are also intimately related to the endocrine system.

---

[11] To learn more read, *The Sathya Sai Speaks*, Volume 10, pages 117-120

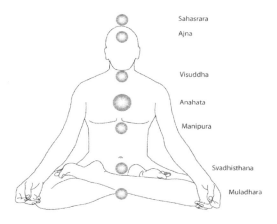

The first chakra is the 'Muladhara', the root chakra, which is the link in each person with 'Prakriti', Mother Nature. This is the lowest chakra and is located at the lower end of the spinal passage. It is related to the annamaya kosha or food body. Muladhara is related to instinct, security, survival, and basic human potentiality.

The next chakra is the 'Svadhisthana', at the point of the navel, and is the guardian of the pranamaya kosha (the vital life force or the breath sheath), the vital facet of the person. It is the fire principle, the spring and source of warmth in the body that maintains the processes of digestion and protection from environmental change. It is connected to reproduction and the vital life force.

The 'Manipura' or the solar plexus chakra is the third sphere of energy. It is the water principle helping the circulation of blood both into the heart and out of it, from all parts of the body. Here, we experience emotional energy. This energy centre holds the key to personal power and growth.

The fourth chakra is the 'Anahata', the heart chakra. It embodies the air principle, which is in charge of the breathing process, inhalation and exhalation, so it is vital for life and activity. It also vitalises the spinal force. This is the chakra of compassion and unconditional love. It is the bridge from personal power to Cosmic (Universal) Power and from materiality to divinity.

The next chakra is the 'Visuddha', the throat chakra, which includes verbal and sound-based consciousness; words, language, art, poetry, music and so on. It plays an important role in understanding dreams, receiving intuition and expressing power. The 'Visuddha' is in the pit of the throat and represents the ether (space) principle.

The sixth chakra or 'Ajna' is located on the mid-brow (also known as the third eye). It is the embodiment of 'Vijnana' (the splendour of awareness). This sphere awakens 'buddhi' (divine intelligence). The 'Ajna' chakra is the passage to the transcendent. When this sphere opens it is easy to recognise that the created world, the world of the senses and the mind, is a dream and that reality is beyond the mind.

Detachment – The Secret to Infinite Peace

The seventh and final energy vortex is the 'Sahasrara', the thousand-petalled lotus at the crown of the head. When the 'Sahasrara' is attained, it is the final consummation of all spiritual practises and all search. The *LiberatingTouch*® Detachment Process incorporates the Chakra Meditation so that you can engage these powerful forces within you to support you on your path to Self- sovereignty.

Using Light Imagery to Uncreate Energetic Links and Purify the Mind

In *LiberatingTouch*®, Light Imagery plays an important part. In Step 3 of the Detachment Process, it is visualised as a laser beam that can take any form to sever and uncreate all energetic links that keep one trapped in reactive behaviour. Later in the same step, Light Imagery is visualised as a waterfall that cleanses, purifies, and washes away all subtle disempowering conditions.

The Tree Integration Meditation

This visualisation is used as the final stage in Step 3 of the *LiberatingTouch*® Detachment Process. This meditation facilitates the experience of becoming one with the Tree, which is the symbol of the Illumined-Self. It is for balancing,

58

integrating, and being nourished by the Cosmic Masculine and Feminine Energies.

There are times when using one or two of these elements will be sufficient to create the necessary healing that you require. However, for more deep-seated attachments, to family, attitudes, trauma, or addictions, it is advisable to practise the complete Detachment Process.

Simon's Experience – Using the Infinity Exercise for Exam Stress

It was a month before my exams, and my mind began to get agitated with the limited time I had left for revision. Within a few days, I also had dreams where people were asking me to help them, and I was refusing them on the grounds that I had enough problems of my own. I knew that I was worried about the exams, and realised that I must be seriously disturbed for it to show at the dream level. However, I tried to ignore this rising panic within me and carried on revising. A week passed in this fashion, but the worry did not let up. I remember thinking that my life was perfect, and I was quite happy, but the only blot in my consciousness was this worry about the approaching exam.

A few days later my younger brother called to say that my older brother had passed away. I felt sad at his passing, but from a spiritual perspective, I understood that no one died, but rather, they moved to a different level of consciousness. However, even this incident seemed minor, compared to the approaching exam. I got to a point two weeks later, where I felt that I was not doing enough, even though I was doing hours of revision. A week before my exam, I had a dream, where the Mother (GOD as the feminine principle) came and said, 'do what you normally do, and hand it over'. I realised that I had the necessary tool, in the form of the 'Infinity Exercise' that could help me become more detached. I immediately started doing the Infinity Exercise to the exam. As I began to practise the exercise, I became less and less affected by what I realised was the fear of failing the exam. In the next few days, I got to a point where I even reduced my revision hours and enjoyed doing other things. I realised that I did not even have to do the complete detachment process for this to work. On the day of the exam, I went and did the exam without any worries. Perhaps, not worrying about the exams helped me to do a better job. It helped me put my thoughts, and understanding of the subject matter on paper. A couple of months later, I got my results, which showed that I had passed my exams.

I find that the tools and processes in LiberatingTouch® extremely powerful as they have helped me. I use the Infinity Exercise regularly to help me become detached in all sorts of difficult situations, where emotions like anger, or frustration, can cloud the mind, thinking or judgement. I also use it when I am on the telephone with other people, as no matter where in the world they are, the Infinity is not limited by distance."

Jemima's Experience – Creating Honesty and Harmony in all Relationships

"I remember the first time Ranjana led me into this process. I was not sure about it, but I was so committed to finding some peace and joy that I would have done anything. The promise of bliss through LiberatingTouch® both intrigued and seduced me, and so the formal Detachment Process began. It is now very much part of my life, from the momentary 'Infinity flows' (when I need some space from a thought, emotion, situation or person), to daily focused practice on some deep-seated obstacle/opportunity between me and love-knowingness-bliss.

Over the past two years, I have faced a lot of personal and professional challenges. Many of the detachments that I completed were with people I work with, with whom I had entangled and complex relationships, which resulted in dysfunctional and difficult interactions. I have done detachments with two of the key players: the company and, most memorably, the 'energy of manipulation'. I have also completed detachments with my parents and to myself as a young child, which could have been an aspect that was holding me in the past. Sometimes I was surprised about what came up for me to detach from, and some processes have been much stronger than others. Writing the letter after the final visualisation has given me a sense of completion and freedom. What comes out in that letter after Step 3 of the Detachment Process is often the most surprising of all, and is when the most honest, heartfelt moments of truth can arise.

When going through Steps 1 and 2 of the complete Detachment Process, I have had a variety of insights and responses depending on the detachment subject. Sometimes, one of the first thoughts I would have on waking would be, 'It's time to detach' and I couldn't wait to start my morning rituals that incorporated the Detachment Process. Other days I would completely forget, and for days at a time. I don't think it was about how busy I was; perhaps it was avoidance, or just me not really acknowledging the need to detach from 'the thing'. I would often have insights during the process, especially during the Finger Holds and sometimes even enter 'the gap' (a space of profound peace) for long periods.

When I was detaching from my work colleagues (they had no idea what I was doing), things often got worse, almost as if they were protesting about having to own their own energy, and not having access to mine to manipulate.

I also had some very deep dreams throughout the processes, which revealed truths, anxieties, and my deepest knowing. They helped me to acknowledge the reality and unreality, or illusion of situations. On completion, most of the processes resulted in tangible changes in my thoughts and circumstances. They were empowering, freeing and resulted in progress on many levels. I have shared this process with many of the students I train, and also with friends and family. I love the process. I am still not 100% on identifying what I need to detach from, and I do need to refine that enquiry aspect.

Thank you for introducing and guiding me through this so many times. Thank you for your commitment, eternal love, and for the joy of experiencing the light of Truth that burns so brightly in me, around me, from me and through me when I practise the many LiberatingTouch® processes."

Angel's Experience – Saying Goodbye

"In July, my husband, Jude, was diagnosed with the return of his cancer as metastasized renal cell carcinoma. It was the start of an emotional roller coaster. At the time, we never realised what truly was about to unfold before us. Our relationship was tattered and torn, and we were both so wounded. We were unable to separate for reasons unknown to us at the time, but I have now discovered that our journey together had not come to an end, and we were to receive one final blessing. This was confirmation to me that our time together walking the planet was a divine plan and was meant to be. We had 3 final months together, and we never wasted a moment.

I can't remember the exact timing, but I think that it was about 8 weeks into Jude's final thirteen weeks when my sister introduced me to the Infinity Symbol. It resonated with me immediately, and I started using it every day following my meditation time. Sometimes I would find myself doodling it. I had a conscious awareness of it all the time. I didn't know then that the power from using this symbol would bring peace to my partner's final moments. In his last days, I was tired; I had been up beside him, loving and nurturing him without sleep for close to fifty-two hours. (As I write this, I realise that fifty-two hours is the same number of hours that I was in labour with our 2nd son, and Jude never left my side. Wow!) During the last fifty-two hours with Jude, I worked on the energy points my sister had taught me and used the Finger Holds. I truly believe right up till those last moments he was releasing. What a privilege that I could give him that opportunity to heal and become complete. In Jude's' last moments, I was drawn to using the small poultice with Rose Oil and trace the Infinity Symbol on his chest. I whispered the words, "It's ok my darling, you are safe. Here baby, take Gods' hand. He is right here with us, and ready to lead you. Go with Love. I will place your hand in God's hand. Oh, my darling you are free". Jude opened his eyes for one last time and looked at me with intense love and no words were needed; it was total gratitude, and his final goodbye to me. I just realised I was not frightened at that moment, and I could truly feel the energy around us. A miracle occurred before our very eyes. I had witnessed the peaceful crossing over to eternity of someone dear to me.

Now I feel more connected to Jude through my detachment than ever before. My love for him is deeper and different. I haven't used the Infinity Symbol since that moment, but now I understand the total simplicity of it. It has the potential to move mountains and create healing beyond our limitations. This symbol will be mine forever."

4.
The Complete
Detachment Process

The LiberatingTouch® Detachment Process has 4 Main Steps

1. Relax, connect, and ask the Illumined-Self what to detach from.
2. Practise the Infinity Exercise with the Finger Holds.
3. Use the Detachment Visualisation audio or script.
4. Write the letter to the SELF.

The first step entails practising the Liquid Light Relaxation and the Tree Meditation, where you connect to the Illumined-Self and ask what you need to detach from. The second step requires that you do the Infinity Exercise and Finger Holds, with whatever you have been given (for a minimum of two weeks). This is necessary to build up the energy to do the third part, which is the Detachment Process guided visualisation meditation. The fourth and final part requires you to write a letter and then burn it. This process enables you to take back your power, which was locked in the object or person, from which you are detaching. You will need all your personal power back, in order, to reconnect with the Cosmic Power.

Step 1: Relax, connect and ask the Illumined-Self what to detach from

Step 1 comprises of three stages. The first stage uses the Liquid Light Relaxation Technique, to assist the seeker[12] to become relaxed and open, in order to connect to the Illumined-Self. In the second stage, the seeker connects to the Illumined-Self via the Tree Meditation, which will enable them to get their thinking, fears, and desires out of the way and entrust the session to the Illumined-Self. In the third stage, the seeker asks the Illumined-Self to show them what they need to detach from, to appear in the opposite loop of the Infinity Symbol.

The seeker begins by making themselves comfortable in a suitable position to help them contemplate. They can either sit on the ground, or in a chair, or in any position that allows them to feel relaxed. They can place one hand above the other in a cupped position, palms facing upwards resting on their lap. This classic hand pose is called the 'dhyana mudra'

---

[12] The seeker represents you or anyone who is willing to work on themselves in order to experience peace and contentment.

67

as seen in many sculptural images of Buddha. Alternatively, they can also place their fingers in the centre of their palm, or choose any hand posture, or mudras of their choice. Now, with their eyes closed and with their focus on their breath, they can initiate the use of the Liquid Light Relaxation Technique.

In this technique, the seeker visualises that their body is hollow and that liquid white light is entering their body, through the soles of their feet. As the level of the liquid white light rises up through their body, from the feet up to their head, they name that part of their body and state that it is relaxed. For example, they could say that, 'Both my feet are filled with liquid light, and the muscles in my feet are relaxed'. That is, they name the part of the body which indicates the area where light is filling their body, and also state that the muscles are relaxed in that area. They then systematically work their way up to the scalp, till their whole body is completely relaxed.

The next stage involves going deep within themselves and visualising a vast space. They then visualise the Tree within this space, which is a symbol of the Illumined-Self[13]. The seeker visualises the Tree with many coloured ribbons flowing down to the ground and selects any one of the ribbons giving it a

---

[13] The Illumined-Self or "Buddhi" represents the infinite intelligence of Love and Truth.

gentle tug. The tug signifies symbolically the connection to the Tree, and therefore, the Illumined-Self.

The seeker then asks the Illumined-Self to send via the ribbon, the energies of Truth, Self-Responsibility, Peace and Love one at a time. They then visualise these positive energies filling them up, and breathing out any negative qualities, back up the ribbon to be transformed by the Illumined-Self.

In the final stage of Step 1, the seeker visualises a large Infinity Symbol and imagines that they are in one loop of the Infinity Symbol, with the other loop unoccupied. The seeker then asks the Illumined-Self to show what they need to detach from in the unoccupied loop. This can show up as a person, symbol, object, image, emotion or text. Whatever appears in the other loop will be what the seeker needs to detach from. It is **essential to trust** what is being shown.

For your convenience, the Guided Visualisation Script for Step 1 with all the stages is included here. You can have someone read this out to you, or download the audio from https://liberatingtouch.com/

The Guided Visualisation Script for Step 1

First, sit down on the ground, or in a chair, or in any position that allows you to feel comfortable. Place your right hand above the left hand in a cupped position, palms facing upwards, with your hands resting on your lap. This classic hand pose is called the 'dhyana mudra'. Alternatively, you can place your fingers in the centre of your palm, or you can choose any hand posture or mudra of your choice.

The Liquid Light Relaxation

Now, close your eyes and focus on your breath. Breathe in and breathe out. Visualise your body as hollow. Imagine that liquid white light is entering the soles of your feet. As the level of the liquid light rises up from the soles of your feet to your ankles, both your feet are now filled with light, and all the muscles in your feet are completely relaxed.

Visualise the liquid white light rising up from your ankles into your calves, so that both your calves are now filled with light, and all the muscles in your calves are completely relaxed.

Visualise the light now entering your knees and thighs, so that both your knees and thighs are now filled with light and all the muscles in your knees and thighs are completely relaxed.

Visualise the light now entering your bottom, groin and waist; so that your bottom, groin and waist are now filled with light, and all the muscles in your bottom, groin and waist are completely relaxed.

Visualise the light now entering your belly, so that your belly is now filled with light, and all the muscles in your belly are completely relaxed.

Visualise the light now entering the whole of your back, so that the whole of your back is now filled with light, and all the muscles in your back are completely relaxed.

Visualise the light now entering your chest, so that your chest is now filled with light, and all the muscles in your chest are completely relaxed.

Visualise the light now entering both your shoulders, so that both your shoulders are now filled with light and all the muscles in your shoulders are completely relaxed.

Visualise the light now entering your arms, so that both your arms are now filled with light and all the muscles in your arms are completely relaxed.

Visualise the light now entering both your hands, so that both your hands are now filled with light and all the muscles in your hands are completely relaxed.

Visualise the light now entering your neck and throat, so that your neck and throat are now filled with light and all the muscles in your neck and throat are completely relaxed.

Visualise the light now entering your jaws, cheeks and mouth; so that your jaws, cheeks and mouth are now filled with light, and all the muscles in your jaws, cheeks and mouth are completely relaxed.

Visualise the light now entering your eyes, forehead, and scalp, so that your eyes, forehead, and scalp are now filled with light.

Your whole body is filled with light and your body is completely relaxed. As you become more and more relaxed, find yourself going deeper and deeper within yourself. Floating very gently, just like a feather, to the very centre or core of your being. When you reach the very centre of your being, imagine a vast space around you, and in this vast space, you will find the Tree, which is the symbol of the Illumined-Self.

The Tree Meditation for Connecting to the Illumined-Self

The Tree has many different coloured ribbons flowing down from the branches to the ground. Pick any one of the coloured ribbons that catches your eye, reach out, take it in your hands and give it a gentle tug. When you tug on the ribbon, feel the resistance coming from the branch of the Tree where it is attached. When you feel this resistance, know that you are connected to the Illumined-Self.

Now that you are connected to the Tree, which represents the Illumined-Self and is the Source of Wisdom and

Love, you can ask the Illumined-Self to send via your ribbon the light of TRUTH. Visualise this quality of Truth filling your whole being as you breathe it in and as you breathe out, visualise any untruth or false beliefs, leaving you with your breath and going up the ribbon to the Tree to be transformed.

Keep inhaling the light of Truth and exhaling untruth or false beliefs. Continue breathing in the light of Truth and breathing out untruth or false beliefs.

Now ask the Illumined-Self to send the energy of SELF-RESPONSIBILITY, and visualise it coming from the Tree via your ribbon, strengthening you as you inhale. You can visualise the energy of Self-Responsibility filling your whole being with mental and physical strength. As you breathe out, visualise any weakness or ignorance leaving you with your exhalation and going through the ribbon to the Tree to be transformed. Keep inhaling the energy of Self-Responsibility and exhaling weakness and ignorance. Continue breathing in the energy of Self-Responsibility and breathing out weakness and ignorance.

Now ask the Illumined-Self to send you the light of PEACE, and visualise this energy coming from the Tree via the ribbon and filling up your whole being with Peace as you breathe it in and as you breathe out, visualise any disharmony, conflict, or negativity that you are ready to release, leaving you with your exhalation and going up the ribbon to the Tree to be transformed.

Keep inhaling the light of Peace and exhaling disharmony, conflict, or negativity. Continue breathing in the light of Peace and breathing out disharmony, conflict, or negativity.

Now, ask the Illumined-Self to send you the energy of LOVE, and visualise it coming from the Tree via your ribbon, filling your whole being with Love as you breathe it in. Exhale any fears, darkness, or resistance within you that you are ready to release, and visualise them moving up the ribbon to the Tree to be transformed.

Continue inhaling the energy of Love and exhaling any fears, darkness, or resistance. Continue breathing in the energy of Love and breathing out fears, darkness, or resistance.

Now focus on your breath, breathing in all the energies of Truth, Self-Responsibility, Peace and Love, from the Illumined-Self, and exhale anything that you are ready to release. Keep breathing out whatever you are ready to release and see it going back up the Tree, back to the Illumined-Self to be transformed. Keep focusing on your breath.

Asking the Illumined-Self what to Detach from
Now give the ribbon a tug to remind you that you are connected to the Illumined-Self. Visualise the Infinity Symbol and imagine that you are sitting or standing in one loop of the Infinity Symbol and the other loop of the Infinity Symbol is unoccupied.

Ask the Illumined-Self to show you what you need to detach from in the other loop of the Infinity Symbol. Accept whatever you are shown, and do not try to reason out why the person, object, symbol, emotion or text is impressed upon you. TRUST the Illumined-Self.

(Pause for a while)

Slowly return to the here and now (time, date and venue). Stretch and ground yourself. Make a note of what you have received and begin with Step 2.

Step 2: Practice the Infinity Exercise with the Finger Holds

Step 2 of the Detachment Process is for building up the energy the seeker requires, to detach and reclaim their personal power. It also helps the seeker to release fear and resistance. Breaking or changing negative habitual conditioning takes a lot of energy, as the old habitual patterns have to dissolve before the new balanced energy can be integrated. This step can be challenging as stored uncomfortable and old impressions surface, ready for clearing.

In this stage of the Detachment Process, the seeker visualises the Infinity Symbol and sees themselves in one of the loops of the Infinity Symbol and whatever the seeker was shown to detach[14] from, in the other loop. The seeker then visualises a 'serpent of light' going along the path of the Infinity Symbol, clockwise around the loop in front of them and then anti-clockwise around the seeker, in a continuous movement.

The movement of the 'serpent of light' in a clockwise direction, in the loop in front of the seeker, creates a vortex of spinning energy in a clockwise direction. Similarly, as the 'serpent of light' goes around the loop the seeker is in, in an anti-clockwise direction, it creates a vortex of energy in an anti-clockwise direction. This movement of energy is formed because the mind is extremely powerful, and hence the adage, "as you think, so it becomes". The very act of visualising the

---

[14] Occasionally, while you are doing the Infinity Exercise whatever you are detaching from may change.

movement of the 'serpent of light' along the path of the Infinity Symbol, instructs the subconscious in symbolic language, to keep the seeker and the object of detachment apart. Also, the vortex of spinning energy will communicate symbolically to the subconscious, the idea that all the energies in the vortex are going to be brought to its centre; just like water spiralling in a washbasin and going down the outflow. This weakens the energetic links between the seeker and the object of detachment. It also builds up the necessary energy required to complete the detachment process, and regain their personal power. For the next 15 days or more, the seeker needs to practise the Infinity Exercise along with the Finger Holds

The Finger Holds

While focusing on the Infinity Exercise, hold your THUMB (either side) and repeat within yourself: "I now release all my anxieties in relation to this ___ (whatever you are detaching from) ___. I am open to perceptive/inspired action."

While focusing on the Infinity Exercise, hold your INDEX finger (either side) and repeat within yourself: "I now release all my fears in relation to this ___ (whatever you are detaching from) ___. I invite Love here."

While focusing on the Infinity Exercise, hold your MIDDLE finger (either side) and repeat within yourself: "I now release all my impatience in relation to this ___ (whatever you are detaching from) ___. I choose Peace."

While focusing on the Infinity Exercise, hold your RING finger (either side) and repeat within yourself: "I now release all my sadness in relation to this ___ (whatever you are detaching from) ___. I welcome Truth."

While focusing on the Infinity Exercise, hold your LITTLE finger (either side) and repeat within yourself: "I now release all my criticisms in relation to this ___ (whatever you are detaching from) ___. I open to serenity"

While focusing on the Infinity Exercise, place your fingers in the centre of your palm (either side) and repeat within yourself: "I now release all my dejection in relation to this ___ (whatever you are detaching from) ___. I choose to identify with constant integrated awareness."

(Refer to pages 53 and 85-87 for more Finger Holds).

Step 3: Use the Detachment Visualisation audio or script

After the seeker has practised the Infinity Exercise for the required time, they will need someone to read the script of the Detachment Visualisation out to them, to complete this Step. Alternatively, they can download the recorded version from the LiberatingTouch website.[15]

---

[15] the audios can be located on https://liberatingtouch.com

Outline for The Detachment Visualisation

- Begin with the Liquid Light Relaxation Technique
- Use the Tree Meditation Technique for connecting to the Illumined-Self and receive the qualities of Truth, Self- Responsibility, Peace and Love
- Revisit the Infinity Exercise
- Use the Finger Holds
- Raise the vibration with the Chakra Meditation
- Use Light Imagery to uncreate energetic links and purify the mind
- Finish with the Tree Integration Technique for balancing, aligning and being nourished by the Cosmic Masculine and Feminine Energies

The Complete Script for the Detachment Visualisation Technique

First sit down on the ground or in a chair, or in any position that allows you to feel comfortable. Place your right hand above the left hand in a cupped position, palms facing upwards, with your hands resting on your lap. This classic hand pose is called the 'dhyana mudra'. Alternatively, you can place your fingers in the centre of your palm, or you can choose any hand posture or mudra of your choice.

The Liquid Light Relaxation

Now, close your eyes and focus on your breath. Breathe in and breathe out. Visualise your body as hollow. Imagine that liquid white light is entering the soles of your feet. As the level of the liquid light rises up from the soles of your feet to your ankles, both your feet are now filled with light and all the muscles in your feet are completely relaxed.

Visualise the liquid white light rising up from your ankles into your calves so that both your calves are now filled with light and all the muscles in your calves are completely relaxed.

Visualise the light now entering your knees and thighs so that both your knees and thighs are now filled with light and all the muscles in your knees and thighs are completely relaxed.

Visualise the light now entering your bottom, groin and waist so that your bottom, groin and waist are now filled with light and all the muscles in your bottom, groin and waist are completely relaxed.

Visualise the light now entering your belly so that your belly is now filled with light and all the muscles in your belly are completely relaxed.

Visualise the light now entering the whole of your back so that the whole of your back is now filled with light and all the muscles in your back are completely relaxed.

Visualise the light now entering your chest so that your chest is now filled with light and all the muscles in your chest are completely relaxed.

Visualise the light now entering both your shoulders so that both your shoulders are now filled with light and all the muscles in your shoulders are completely relaxed.

Visualise the light now entering your arms so that both your arms are now filled with light and all the muscles in your arms are completely relaxed.

Visualise the light now entering both your hands so that both your hands are now filled with light and all the muscles in your hands are completely relaxed.

Visualise the light now entering your neck and throat so that your neck and throat are now filled with light and all the muscles in your neck and throat are completely relaxed.

Visualise the light now entering your jaws, cheeks and mouth so that your jaws, cheeks and mouth are now filled with light, and all the muscles in your jaws, cheeks and mouth are completely relaxed.

Visualise the light now entering your eyes, forehead and scalp so that your eyes, forehead and scalp are now filled with light.

Your whole body is filled with light and your body is completely relaxed. As you become more and more relaxed find yourself going deeper and deeper within yourself. Floating very gently, just like a feather, to the very centre or core of your being. When you reach the very centre of your being imagine a vast space around you. In this space, you will find the Tree, which is the symbol of the Illumined-Self.

The Tree Meditation for Connecting to the Illumined-Self

The Tree has many different coloured ribbons flowing down from the branches to the ground. Pick any one of the coloured ribbons that catches your eye, take it in your hands and give it a gentle tug. When you tug on the ribbon, feel the resistance coming from the branch of the Tree, where it is attached. When you feel this resistance know that you are connected to the Illumined-Self.

Now that you are connected to the Tree, which represents the Illumined-Self and is the Source of Wisdom and

83

Detachment – The Secret to Infinite Peace

Love, you can ask the Illumined-Self to send via your ribbon **Truth**. Visualise this quality of Truth filling your whole being as you breathe it in and as you breathe out, visualise any untruth or false beliefs, leaving you with your breath and going up the ribbon to the Tree to be transformed.

Keep inhaling Truth and exhaling untruth or false beliefs. Continue breathing in Truth and breathing out untruth or false beliefs.

Now ask the Illumined-Self to send you the energy of **Self-Responsibility**, and visualise it coming from the Tree via your ribbon, strengthening you as you inhale. You can visualise the energy of Self-Responsibility filling your whole being with mental and physical strength. As you breathe out, visualise any weakness or ignorance leaving you with your exhalation and going up the ribbon to the Tree to be transformed. Keep inhaling the energy of Self-Responsibility and exhaling weakness and ignorance. Continue breathing in the energy of Self-Responsibility and breathing out weakness and ignorance.

Now ask the Illumined-Self to send you **Peace** and visualise this energy coming from the Tree via the ribbon and filling up your whole being with Peace as you breathe it in. As you breathe out, visualise any disharmony, conflict, or negativity that you are ready to release, leaving you with your exhalation and going up via the ribbon to the Tree to be transformed.

Keep inhaling Peace and exhaling disharmony, conflict, or negativity. Continue breathing in Peace and breathing out disharmony, conflict, or negativity.

Now ask the Illumined-Self to send you **Love** and visualise it coming down from the Tree via your ribbon, filling your whole being with Love as you breathe it in. Exhale any fears, darkness, or resistance within you that you are ready to release and visualise it going back up the ribbon to the Tree to be transformed. Continue inhaling Love and exhaling any fears, darkness, or resistance. Continue breathing in Love and breathing out fears, darkness, or resistance.

Now focus on your breath, breathing in all the energies of Truth, Self-Responsibility, Peace and Love from the Illumined-Self, and exhale anything that you are ready to release. Keep breathing out whatever you are ready to release and see it going back up the Tree, back to the Illumined-Self to be transformed. Keep focusing on your breath.

The Infinity Exercise

Now visualise the Infinity Exercise that you have been practising. Imagine that you are sitting or standing in one of the loops of the Infinity Symbol, whichever is comfortable for you, and visualise 'the person, symbol, or object' that you have been detaching from in the opposite loop. Visualise the white serpent of light moving along the path of the Infinity Symbol. Watch this serpent-like energy moving faster and faster with increasing power. Continue visualising this white serpent of light moving along the path of the Infinity Symbol for a few minutes, while doing the Finger Holds.

The Finger Holds

While focusing on the Infinity Exercise, hold your THUMB (either side) and repeat within yourself: "I now release all my anxieties in relation to this ___ (whatever you are detaching from) ___ . I am open to experiencing Self-Responsibility and I am developing positive boundaries in relation to this."

While focusing on the Infinity Exercise, hold your INDEX finger (either side) and repeat within yourself: "I now release all my fears in relation to this ___ (whatever you are detaching from) ___ . I am open to experiencing Love and I am discovering creative solutions in relation to this."

Detachment – The Secret to Infinite Peace

While focusing on the Infinity Exercise, hold your MIDDLE finger (either side) and repeat within yourself: "I now release all my frustrations in relation to this ___ (whatever you are detaching from) ___. I am open to experiencing Peace and I am regaining my equanimity (balance) in relation to this."

While focusing on the Infinity Exercise, hold your RING finger (either side) and repeat within yourself: "I now release all my sadness in relation to this ___ (whatever you are detaching from) ___. I am open to experiencing Truth and I am aware of exhaling my old belief systems in relation to this."

While focusing on the Infinity Exercise, hold your LITTLE finger (either side) and repeat within yourself: "I now release all my struggle in relation to this ___ (whatever you are detaching from) ___. I am open to experiencing Serenity and I am developing effortless understanding in relation to this."

While focusing on the Infinity Exercise, place your fingers in the centre of your palm (either side) and repeat within yourself: "I now release all my despondency in relation to this ___ (whatever you are detaching from) ___. I am open to experiencing Fulfilment, Integration and I am cultivating relationships based on Truth."

The Chakra Meditation

Give the ribbon a tug to remind you that you are connected to the Illumined-Self. Remember the Infinity Exercise, and what you are detaching from. Focus on your breath, breathing in and breathing out. Now we will do the chakra meditation to raise the vibration.

Imagine or visualise the first chakra, the 'muladhara', at the base of your spine. The colour of this energy vortex is red. Imagine taking a red thread of light from this sphere of energy, and guide it up your spine towards the next chakra in the pelvic region.

This chakra in your pelvic region is the 'svadhisthana', and it is orange in colour. Take an orange thread of light from this sphere of energy, twist it around the red thread of light, and guide it up your spine to the third chakra in the solar plexus region.

The third chakra in your solar plexus is the 'manipura', and it is yellow in colour. Take a yellow thread of light from this sphere of energy, twist it around the red and orange threads of light, and guide it up your spine towards the fourth chakra in the middle of your sternum.

The fourth chakra, the 'anahata', also known as the heart chakra, is green in colour. Take a green thread of light from this sphere of energy, twist it around the red, orange and yellow threads of light, and guide it up the spine to the fifth chakra located in the throat area.

The fifth chakra, the 'visuddha', is blue in colour. Take a blue thread of light from this sphere of energy, and twist it around the red, orange, yellow and green threads of light, and guide it up to the sixth chakra located in the forehead.

The sixth chakra, the 'ajna ', is also known as the third eye and is violet in colour. Take a violet thread of light and weave it with all the other threads of light; the red, orange, yellow, green and blue, and visualise them all twirled around as one rope of light, rising up through the seventh chakra, also known as the 'sahasrara', or crown chakra.

Visualise this rope of light coming out of the top of your head as a fountain of white light. Imagine this fountain of white light pouring out from the top of your head, and falling to the

Detachment – The Secret to Infinite Peace

ground around you in a curtain of light, spinning very gently around you. As you visualise it, hear the sound of 'Aum'; the sound of creation, resounding within you with every breath you take.

Keep visualising the fountain of light spinning around you, and experience the sound of 'Aum' vibrating within you. Allow your vibration to align with the resonance of the 'Aum'.

Light Imagery to Uncreate Energetic Links

Give your ribbon a gentle tug and remind yourself that you are connected to the Illumined-Self. Visualise the Infinity Exercise that you have been practising. Now imagine 'the person, symbol, or object'[16] that you have been detaching from in the opposite loop of the Infinity Symbol. Visualise the white serpent of light moving along the path of the Infinity Symbol. Watch this serpent-like energy move faster and faster, with increasing power.

Ask the Illumined-Self to send down a laser beam of light now. This light can take the shape or form of any object, for example, a sword of light. Let this light move along the path of the Infinity Symbol. As this light travels around the Infinity Symbol, it severs and dissolves all energetic links between you

---

[16] When reading this script, you can replace the words, 'person, symbol, or object', with the description or name if you know what the seeker is detaching from.

and what you are detaching from. Continue watching this laser beam of light moving along the path of the Infinity Symbol, uncreating any mental-emotional energetic links between you and 'the person, symbol, or object' in the other half of the Infinity Symbol.

As this laser beam of light moves along the path of the Infinity Symbol, it uncreates and unmakes any conditions or patterns between you and 'the person, symbol, or object' in the other half of the Infinity Symbol.

Keep watching this laser beam of light moving along the path of the Infinity Symbol, and as it moves along the path of the Infinity Symbol, it uncreates and dissolves all energetic links, whether it is visible or invisible, between you and 'the person, symbol, or object' in the other half of the Infinity Symbol. All energetic links between you and whatever you are detaching from is now severed, dissolved, and uncreated. There are no more energetic links between you and whatever you are detaching from.

(Pause for a while)

You can ask the Illumined-Self to appear as a Mentor and take 'the person, symbol, or object', or you can place the symbol or object at the foot of the Tree. If it is a person, you can visualise leading them to the Tree so that they merge with the Tree. Visualise or imagine that the Illumined-Self has removed whatever you have been detaching from in the other loop so that

Detachment – The Secret to Infinite Peace

there is nothing left in that loop. Thank the Illumined-Self for enabling you to have the lessons that you need to go forward in your journey. If you need to forgive or ask for forgiveness, you can do this now.

(Pause for a while)

Once this is complete, see the serpent of light return and dissolve into the Tree. Now ask the Illumined-Self to rain light upon you like a waterfall, washing away all conditions and patterns connected to 'the person, symbol, or object'. The waterfall of light dissolves and transforms all tendencies and habits related to 'the person, symbol, or object'. Continue inhaling this light and exhaling any related patterns and conditions. Feel your body, mind and life being bathed in this light, cleansing any remaining tendencies within you and removing all latent inclinations and subtle habits you may have adopted from, or in response to, 'the person, symbol, or object'. Feel the healing taking place as your conditions and patterns transform and allow you to regain your power. With every breath, reclaim and regain your power. Keep inhaling the light, and exhaling any remaining subtle disempowering conditions relating to 'the person, symbol, or object'. Experience the inhale and the exhale balancing. Now, step into your power, and see yourself shining and radiant with Love and Truth.

The Tree Integration Meditation

Give your ribbon a gentle tug and remind yourself that you are connected to the Illumined-Self. Visualise yourself going up to the Tree and stand or sit with your back against its trunk, knowing it will support you. Identify with the Tree. Visualise your energy field and the energy field of the Tree, merging together to become one. Feel yourself become one with the Tree. Imagine that you are sending your roots down deep into Mother Earth, like the Tree does, to bring up the nourishment you need from the Cosmic Mother. Inhale whatever you need, such as love, affection, acceptance, compassion and acknowledgement, or anything else you think you lack and breathe out any negative emotions which you are willing to release. Now continue breathing in all the energies and breathing out whatever you are ready to release. Focus on your breath and keep breathing in all the nourishing energies and breathing out whatever you are ready to release.

Reach up as the Tree does with its branches and leaves towards the sun, the Cosmic Father, and breathe in whatever is being given to you from that source of nourishment. Exhale anything that could prevent you from receiving it. You may want to specify what you wish to be given, such as courage, validation, acceptance, affection, protection and support, or anything else that comes to your mind. As you breathe out, let go of any negative emotions that you are willing to release. Now keep breathing in all the energies and breathing out whatever you are inspired to release. Focus on your breath and continue breathing in all the positive energies and breathing out whatever you are ready to release.

Now inhale from both sources and with each breath, feel the two streams of nourishment flow throughout your body, bringing about the balance you need between the Yin and Yang forces of the earth and sun. Stay connected in this way, breathing in whatever you are being given. This unification with the Tree, energises, revitalises and heals you.

(Pause for a while)

You can return to the Tree at any time to seek guidance, nourishment and healing. We end this meditation by thanking the Illumined-Self.

"May all the worlds be blessed with happiness, peace and contentment."

Now, slowly return to the here and now (time, date and venue). Stretch and ground yourself.

Step 3 is now concluded.

Step 4: *Write the Letter to the SELF*

In this last step, the seeker writes a letter to the SELF, stressing what they learnt from their experience, and to express their gratitude. The seeker affirms their newfound freedom. After the seeker has done this, they need to burn the letter. The fire is used as a metaphorical postal service to the SELF.

Here is an example of a letter. This is a rough guide. It is essential for the seeker to write this letter in their own words:

Beloved SELF,

Thank you for assisting me in detaching from this person/situation/habit/energy... and freeing me to live in... Love and Truth...

Thank you for the lessons of.... And for helping me integrate all that I have learnt.

Help me forgive.... So that I am now free to grow.

Thank you for this healing and for restoring my power to me... Help me integrate this now.

Yours,

The seeker

After writing the letter, burn the letter, then add some water to the ashes and pour this in a tree or shrub, let it return to nature.

Important Considerations

In Step 1, if you do not get a clear indication from the Illumined-Self what to detach from, you can:

1. Ask a *LiberatingTouch*® Facilitator for help.
2. Begin the process by detaching from one of your parents.
3. Start with what is causing you the most tension in your life now.
4. Wait a few days and ask again. Go with whatever you are shown. You do not need to understand it; TRUST whatever the Illumined-Self has shown you.

You can detach from almost anything, but there are exceptions to the rule. If you are married, then you can use the Infinity Exercise, but do not use the full *LiberatingTouch*® Detachment Process with your spouse. If you are divorced, separated, or a widower, then use the complete *LiberatingTouch*® Detachment Process to detach from your ex-partner. The other exception is for children under the age of puberty; we recommend that you do not use the full *LiberatingTouch*® Detachment Process with your child until she/he has reached puberty. However, you can use the Infinity Exercise to create space and prevent negative emotional reactions with your child. You can teach your child the infinity exercise. It is a safe and useful resource for children.

Another common error is to try and detach from everything at once. There is the temptation to use the complete process on all your issues in one go. This is not efficient as it takes a lot of energy to detach and trying to do too many in one go makes the process ineffective. Do the *LiberatingTouch*® Detachment Process to any one person, issue, or symbol, one at a time according to your guidance. In the meantime, you can use the Infinity Exercise to create space with all your other concerns.

Frequently Asked Questions

"Detachment is not disconnection from the world around us. It is loving connection without suffering. Detachment helps us experience unity and harmony in thoughts, words and actions."

Why do we need to detach?

We need to detach from attachments and desires to be able to liberate ourselves from the cycle of birth and death. We have created these attachments through our experiences in many lives. We need to free the energy locked in the conditioned processes that manifest as attachments to people and things of the world, in order to increase our personal power. Only through recovering our personal power, can we connect to the Cosmic Power which is GOD. Also, when we become progressively more detached, we will be able to live in the world joyfully as the push and pull of attachments and desires do not control our emotions (i.e. unfulfilled desires can create sorrow).

Are there any healing reactions to the Detachment Process?

When people are in stressful situations for instance, when they are irritated by someone or something, no matter the distance, and they use the Infinity Exercise, most people experience relief. However, when practising the full Detachment Process, some people experience emotional intensity and uncomfortable insights as old issues, energetic links, old patterns or conditions break down. The energy is released as a dark cloud in the mind, which may appear like depression. This feeling is the result of the mind being used as a crucible to transform the energy from the old patterns or conditions. Once the Detachment Process is complete, these sensations will disappear and one is left with resolution, freedom, and a depth of understanding.

If I detach from my family will I stop caring for them?

No. On the contrary, you would be more unconditional in your love for them. The reactions that you would normally experience with your family would become less or even non-existent. Detachment is a concept that is misunderstood, as it has been confused with not caring. For example, when Eddie did the Detachment Process to his mother, his mother's response to him when he spoke to her after the process, was to tell him that she loved him. She had not said this since he was a little child. Her reaction to his other siblings did not change. What had happened was his proactive endeavour in doing the Detachment Process made a change within him which reflected in the external world. His mother did not change, as she had not made any effort, and this is reflected in her attitude to Eddie's siblings. For instance, when you detach from your parents you are detaching from everything related to them, like their unfulfilled hopes and desires, which they are projecting onto you. This would allow you to be true to yourself and also love them unconditionally.

What is the point of the Infinity Exercise?

The Infinity Exercise has two functions. First, to draw your energy (power) back to yourself, allowing you to respond to all situations and persons with peace and confidence. The second reason is to acquire enough power to finish the complete Detachment Process, effectively. In many cultures and philosophies, God (SELF) is experienced and described as Infinite. The Infinity Symbol is used to remind us that by focusing on the infinite power of the SELF, we can detach with ease. The serpent of light that flows in the path of the Infinity Symbol represents the power of God. This serpent of light helps us create space between reactive elements in our mind, relationships and life, without judging any of them. Everything exists within the SELF. By practising this one simple exercise, we remind ourselves that attachments, desires, or fears, are all energies simply passing through, there is no need for us to get stuck or entangled.

How does the 'Infinity Exercise' work?

The mind is extremely powerful and thoughts can manifest energetically (as you think so it becomes). When you think of the 'white serpent of light' moving along the path of the 'infinity symbol', in a clockwise direction in front of you in your visualisation, then a vortex spinning in a clockwise direction will be created and then when it comes round the loop you are sitting or standing in, it will create a vortex moving in an anticlockwise direction around you. Thus, two energetic vortices will be created, spinning in opposite directions. Physics tells us that objects spinning in opposite directions cannot come together but will pull apart. A vortex will also pull everything to its centre, just like water in a sink which spirals as it drains out. When we do this exercise, we are communicating to the subconscious in symbolic language, to deprogram our attachment to the object, person or symbol in the loop opposite us. Therefore, the subconscious will free the energy locked in the conditioned process and allow us to reclaim back our power. This exercise can be used whenever you feel that you are reacting to someone or something, even during a phone call or when conversing with someone. All you have to do is put yourself in one loop of the infinity symbol and the person or object in the other loop and visualise the 'white serpent of light' going along the path of the 'infinity symbol', till your reaction stops or till you experience calm.

I am detaching from someone; can I also help them?

Yes, you can use the Tree Meditation. You can visualise the person you are detaching from receiving a ribbon and being connected to the Tree. The illustration below will help. Imagine that you are both connected to the Tree with ribbons and so both of you are receiving the nourishing energies from the Illumined-Self. At the same time, you can continue with the Detachment Process knowing that the person is receiving all that they need. Remember, when you free yourself, you free the other person.

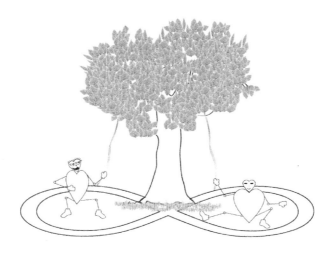

Can I use the Infinity Exercise to help my family (surrogately)?

Yes, you can. You can visualise your family in one loop, and whatever is affecting them in the other loop. This process should not be used to control someone. The consequences can rebound on you if it is abused. Any action intending to control another person would create a response on a karmic level.

I am not comfortable with doing the Chakra meditation, is there an alternative?

If you or your clients are uncomfortable with the Chakra Meditation, then you can use this alternative suggestion. In the Complete Script for the Detachment Visualisation Technique, remove the Chakra Meditation and insert these additional Finger Holds instead.

While focusing on the Infinity Exercise, hold your THUMB (either side) and repeat within yourself: "I now release my resistance to being grounded and open to the healing power of the earth."

While focusing on the Infinity Exercise, hold your INDEX finger (either side) and repeat within yourself: "I now release my resistance to being creative and open to the healing power in nature."

While focusing on the Infinity Exercise, hold your MIDDLE finger (either side) and repeat within yourself: "I now release my resistance to purifying my thinking and open to the healing power in my breath."

While focusing on the Infinity Exercise, hold your RING finger (either side) and repeat within yourself: "I now release my resistance to Love and open to the healing power within me."

While focusing on the Infinity Exercise, hold your LITTLE finger (either side) and repeat within yourself: "I now release my resistance to expressing Truth and open to the healing power of loving communication."

While focusing on the Infinity Exercise, place your fingers in the centre of your palm (either side) and repeat within yourself: "I now release my resistance to reclaiming my power and open to the healing power of clear vision."

Once you have made the replacement, you can return to the section, 'Light Imagery to Uncreate Energetic Links' of the complete Detachment Process.

How long do I need to practise the Infinity Exercise to experience relief?

Everybody and every situation differ, thus there are no guidelines regarding time. Trust your intuition to guide you.

Is one detachment sufficient? Or do I need to do more?

The Infinity Exercise and the Detachment Process helps to keep your mind clean and clear. If we use the analogy of your home, you need to clean your home regularly and clear the rubbish out to enjoy life at home. Similarly, the infinity exercise can be described as keeping your mind clean, if you do it regularly you will notice that you react less and respond more. The Detachment process can be compared to getting rid of the mental clutter of unhappy tendencies and behaviours and so creating space for you to create a life that brings you joy. It is your choice how clean or clear you wish your mind to be. We recommend getting into the habit of practising the infinity exercise as when you feel triggered and use the Detachment Process to bring about positive change.

When the Illumined Self guides you to do more, it is because there are more aspects to the core issues. Therefore, you need to detach from all the aspects in order to clear the core issue that troubles you. So, ask the Illumined Self and go with the guidance.

I have recurring financial problems, and I am in debt, can this help me?

Yes, it can. Start by using the Infinity Exercise to debt, and then use the complete *LiberatingTouch*® Detachment Process. We have had clients that could not find employment and those with financial problems who have used this process. In both cases, the clients overcame their problems. Do get in touch with a *LiberatingTouch*® Facilitator for more advice.

I have been diagnosed with a serious disease can this help me?

Yes, it can. This process can help you cope with the emotional stress of the diagnosis. Start by using the Infinity

Exercise to your diagnosis, and then use the complete *LiberatingTouch*® Detachment Process. Use the processes to help you meet the physical challenge with kindness. Do get in touch with a *LiberatingTouch*® Facilitator for more advice.

I am depressed and anxious; will it help me?

Yes, it can. Start by using the Infinity Exercise to your anxious thoughts to help you overcome the power they have over you. Later, use the complete *LiberatingTouch*® Detachment Process to resolve your problem. Do get in touch with a *LiberatingTouch*® Facilitator for more advice.

Why do I struggle and resist detachment?

The fact is most of us have not been taught to be detached, as we are taught to be attached to our families, friends, possessions, beliefs and so on. We have invested a lot of energy in our attachments over a long period of time, and in many lifetimes. It is only natural that our minds will resist to begin with, and it can feel like a battle. However, with practice, it will get easier. By deciding to reclaim our power from attachments, we are changing centuries of conditioning. We are choosing infinite peace instead of perpetual war. By practising detachment, we transform our lives and the world around us.

Can I skip Step One of the Detachment Process, I know what I want to detach from?

It is important to ask the Illumined Self what to detach from. It may not be what you want to detach from, but it will be what you need to detach from and that in turn will help you with what you want most effectively and efficiently. We strongly advise that you do Step 1. And do the process with whatever you get, even if it seems positive, random, unknown. It doesn't matter, the Illumined Self, your innate wisdom knows how best to help you.

I didn't do Step Four; will that make a difference?

Yes, it will. It is absolutely vital to do Step 4 of the Detachment Process. Without this, the process is incomplete and you will feel it hanging over you. You must write the letter, burn it, and then add some water to the ashes, and pour it at the base of a tree.

Ok so I'll share this in case I'm not the only one... is it just me or am I doing it 'wrong'? My detachments are not quite so clear in terms of their title, nor do I ever/always get a clear link as to what the overarching 'theme' is. I have often found myself being guided to detach from objects or patterns e.g. paintbrush or butterfly or a treasure chest or specific vortices, items I associate with people or events or actions but

rarely do I get to connect it up/ translate it into the much wider theme. Is that the next level up in the art of understanding detachment or have I just not been paying attention properly?! May I ask Ranjana if your guidance is to detach from specific words or from something else? And is it from experience that you can acknowledge and identify that the detachment comes from an overarching theme? With such huge themes you're covering, I feel like it puts my efforts to shame! and without making the connection I somehow feel I'm missing out.**

It is important not to compare your detachment journey with anyone else's. Your communication with the Illumined Self is unique to you. You are not doing it 'wrong'. If you are connecting to the **Illumined Self (IS)** asking what to detach from and going with it, then you are doing it right. The Illumined Self knows how much information we can handle without excessive resistance. In the process, the images, what we get guided to detach from, changes through years of practice. It is not a race.

Before I launch into the lengthy answer, I want to ask you and everyone reading this, what was the reason you started to use the detachment process? Did the purpose change over the years? Do you experience any shifts after completing the process? Have you found it beneficial? What inspires you to continue?

One of my regrets about the detachments that I have completed over the last 25 years or so is that I did not keep a detachment journal. I began to play with the process in my early 20's and at that time, it was because I was struggling with constant anxiety, addictions, uncertainty, fatigue and stress. I was desperate and I needed help and the processes we have outlined in this book empowered me. In the early days, we did not connect to the Illumined Self and ask what to detach from, we decided, and we were encouraged to work through issues with family and friends first before traversing down the route of stuck energies, symbols or patterns. What Eddie and I noticed is that people would work through similar issues repeatedly because they were using their will power and not connecting with the Illumined Self to find the most efficient and effective path forward. We introduced the idea of asking the Illumined Self what we need to detach from, and this completely transformed the work, i.e. the shifts were deeper, lasting and more meaningful.

As I began to ask the Illumined Self what I needed to detach from, I got images, symbols, people, places, ideas and only recently (in the last 4 years) concepts and themes. There have been times when I had no idea what I was detaching from, it felt quite random, but each time after a few days, it felt like another layer that separated me from the SELF dissolved and I accessed more of 'my' True Nature. Sometimes, it was a person, perhaps someone I knew, or someone I did not know like a movie star, or a character from a book, an object like a ladder, a colour, an event, a dream, a desire, a logo... it could be anything, sometimes it was clear and other times not so clear. The Illumined-Self knows that the mind is a master of distraction and resistance, and it knows that love and gentleness are what will heal the mind and induce the mind to want to become an instrument that reflects Love and Truth. Eventually, the mind becomes a flute, in the hands of Love and Truth, capable of expressing the exquisite music of the SELF. The detachment process utilises the capacity of the mind to purify (heal) the mind of lifetimes (if you do not believe in lifetimes, you can say aeons of genetic conditioning) of suffering, limitation, confusion and misunderstanding.

At first, you are working to clear your personal challenges and to empower yourself and as you become clearer, the Illumined Self will guide you to work with issues that impact the whole and this will reveal further personal limitations. You start to work through issues that impact the whole and yourself. I remember one detachment where I saw a naked woman, pregnant and chained to the kitchen sink, it was a tough one, I felt I was working through generations of female pain. I remember for a few years Eddie and I worked on the same detachments at the same time, as the issues impacted us both. Another big detachment was to

Detachment – The Secret to Infinite Peace

inappropriate chatter and I think that had several aspects, images and symbols. One detachment was to a wounded 'Gollum like' feminine figure, I still don't know for sure what she was, perhaps a wounded unloved shadow aspect. What I do know is that when doing that particular detachment, I constantly had waves of anger and grief. On step 3 she transformed into a beautiful nature being and dissolved into the Tree with joy. Perhaps it was an aspect of the wounded earth? Soon after the detachment, I found my relationship with nature deepen. I wish had noted the details of some of these detachments because it is hard to pull them up from memory and I cannot vouch for the accuracy of my recollections.

To begin with, my greatest gain was a shift in my reactivity with those around me, a growing sense of peace within, I found that my addictive obsessive behaviour shifted, and it became easier to be flexible and open to life. I wanted more... greater understanding, love flowing to and from me, freedom from all fear and so here I am persisting, purifying and merging into Truth, being Love. I believe that my detachments are much clearer now, because I am. I am ready to work through and understand how consciousness gets trapped in the drama of desire and attachment. How negative nurture impacts and taints our true nature. The detachment process is a very powerful tool to transform consciousness so that humanity can wake up to the plight it is in and discover that we

Detachment – The Secret to Infinite Peace

can Love ourselves whole. Love alone heals, detachment is your true wealth, awareness of unity is the basis of Truth and knowing the SELF (Creator Source) gives purpose and meaning to life. Detachment is not disconnection from the world around us it is loving connection without suffering. It is the essence of Love. To the infected wounds of attachment, detachment is both the sharp scalpel of Truth required to remove toxins and the soothing balm of Love's healing touch. And sometimes we are not aware of what is festering within. The more detachments we do, the greater our awareness and awakening. As you practice detachment, your awareness will evolve, and you have access to greater understanding.

Doing the complete detachment process is a bit like having a psychological enema/ colonic, not quite comfortable, but great after. Eddie my Beloved Detachment Guru, is always reminding me to infinitise, relax, witness, become aware of the consequences of my thoughts, words and actions, utilise common (divine) sense, investigate every story, emotion and desire with unflinching honesty.

Attachment resonates with denial, resistance, reaction and lack of awareness. The Illumined Self, which is omnipotent, guides us with love, so we engage in the process of letting go and allowing detachment. The Illumined-Self has your number and knows how to get through to you. Detachment is the most misunderstood principle (sacred law) of life. Self-confidence is reliant on the consistent practice of detachment. As we grow in confidence, we experience love, this fills us with peace, and opens our awareness to the truth, so that we can know bliss, which is the SELF.

How can I learn more about this process?

This book is a comprehensive foundational guide to help you understand attachment and how to detach. However, to know more about the process of detachment, it would be advisable to speak with a *LiberatingTouch*® Facilitator. You can find one at: https://liberatingtouch.com

An Important Note About the Illumined-Self

You will notice that there is a fair bit of mention about the **Illumined-Self (IS)**, formerly referred to as the Higher-Self, in this book. In Truth, it is the connection to the Illumined Self that makes *LiberatingTouch*® work the way it does.

When we speak of the Illumined-Self, we are referring to the reflection of God or the Infinite Intuitive Self that exists through all time and space in every being (When we speak of GOD, we mean the nameless, formless, ONE – known in the Vedas as Brahman). There is only the one Illumined-Self – **the reflection** of The Totality - the Absolute Omnipotent Self – Absolute Truth from which Infinite Love emerges. The

Absolute Self is beyond Consciousness – beyond light and dark, beyond love, beyond duality and non-duality, it has no beginning or end, AS IT **IS**, IT **IS**. The Illumined Self is a result of the Absolute Self projecting IT Self into Creation. In the past, we called the Illumined-Self the Higher-Self, but this is a misnomer, it would be better served to call it THAT, the Infinite Intelligent Intuitive Self (IIIS, there are many teachers who refer to their experience of oneness with the Illumined Self as Is-ness). In some of the most ancient texts, it is written that there are as many names and forms of God as there are life forms. But they are all One and the same Illumined Self. There is only One Illumined-Self that can reveal itself through all names and forms.

      The Illumined Self, the One, communes with each one of us uniquely, exquisitely, perfectly. It is a Heart to Heart, a One to One connection, there are no intermediaries. Sometimes the Illumined Self gets others to confirm our experience and knowing, helping us discriminate and discern the mind's chatter and the Illumined Self Truth.

About Ranjana and Eddie

In the last 25 years or so, Eddie and Ranjana have been exploring and developing processes for health, and spiritual regeneration so that their clients and students can be free to create and embrace the life that reflects the fullness and potential of who they are.

Ranjana is an inspired and sensitive educator and holistic health professional. She is also an artist, writer and health researcher. She has travelled extensively and lectured in Fine Arts. Ranjana succeeded in overcoming chronic health challenges using the innovative techniques and healing modalities that she now imparts. She supports her clients with enlightening understanding and her love for Truth.

Eddie is an intuitive instructor, therapist and self-taught musician. He has the innate ability to sense disharmony and restore balance with astute insight. His many years of experience working with clients have helped him understand that each person has a unique story and unlimited potential. By unravelling the meaning in their stories, he brings clarity and empowers his clients.

Together they create a nurturing and dynamic space for their clients and students to heal, reclaim their power, become self-confident, and eventually Self-Realise. One of the effective methods that they use repeatedly is the *LiberatingTouch®* Detachment Process and all its variations.

Eddie and Ranjana attribute all their insights, experiences, inspiration and gifts with deep gratitude to their Spiritual Master, Sri Sathya Sai Baba.

"Our purpose with this book is to help you discover that you can reclaim your power, you can experience limitless peace and you can know the Truth underlying your existence. Once you experience this Truth, there is no turning back; the Truth eventually consumes you, annihilating fear, desire, and attachments one at a time with infinite Love." – Ranjana and Eddie

Detachment – The Secret to Infinite Peace

Printed in Great Britain
by Amazon